The Stories of Emmy
A Girl Like Heidi

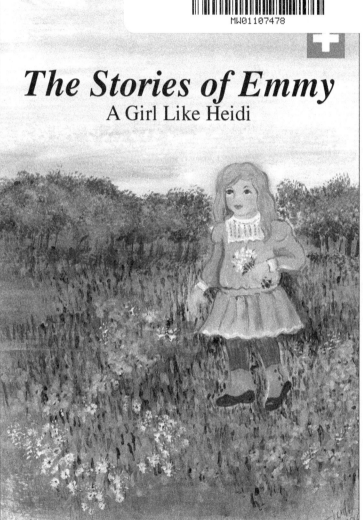

by
Doris Smith Naundorf

The Stories of Emmy
A Girl Like Heidi
by Doris Smith Naundorf

Printed in the United States of America

ISBN 9781609578800

Unless otherwise indicated, Bible quotations are taken from
The Nelson Study Bible, New King James Version. Copyright
© 1997 by Thomas Nelson Publishers.

Jesus Blesses Little Children
Mark 10:13 – 16
Then they brought little children to Him that
He might touch them; but the disciples rebuked those
who brought them. But when Jesus saw it, He was greatly
displeased and said to them. "Let the little ones come to
Me, and do not forbid them, for of such is the kingdom of
God. Assuredly I say to you, whoever does not receive the
kingdom of God as a little child, will by no means enter it."
And He took them up in His arms, and laid His
hands on them, and blessed them.

The artist of the painting of Emmy on the front cover
is Judi Cermak of Canandaigua, New York. She is a retired
art teacher at the Bloomfield, New York School District,
and a well-known artist in Canandaigua.

www.xulonpress.com

Table of Contents

Foreword

Welcome to **The Stories of Emmy** which are anecdotes my mother told me when I was a little girl. I think of *Emmy* as a real-life *Heidi* growing up in the Swiss-German area of Switzerland. Emmy's family lived in a village near the city of *Basel*. They spoke *Baseldeutsch*, a particular dialect spoken in and around that city. To honor them, I chose to use a few words or phrases from their dialect to make the stories authentically Swiss. The words are shown in italics. Some of the words you'll know as you read along – *Vatti* is Father, *Mutti* is Mother, *Grossmutti* is Grandmother. Other words are not so easily known, so I've included them in a glossary at the end of the book. Happy memories have been revived as I have used words that I learned during my own childhood.

Here are a few facts about life in Switzerland to help you place yourself in the stories. The Confederation of Switzerland, slightly larger than our U.S. state of Connecticut, is more than 700 years old. Each of the cantons (states) has its own particular dialect.

In 1905, as today, German was spoken in formal situations. Swiss-German children in a primary school talked with each other and their teachers in their dialect. During their class in High German — which is still their written language — they spoke in German. Children in Emmy's class began to learn the formal language so that in two or three years they would be prepared to discover the rich literature for children in High German. This is true for Swiss children now in school.

Still other sections of the country have dialects of French (21 percent) and Italian (4 percent). Also there is a special language called Romansh (1 percent) in the Grisons, a tiny section in the southeast of the country.

Acknowledgments

To confirm the vocabulary, I have used Rudolf Suter's **Baseldeutsch-Wörterbuch**, second revision and expanded edition, published by Christoph Merian Verlag, Basel, Switzerland. This dictionary is a treasured gift to me from Professor Dr. Anneleis Häcki Berhofer, University of Basel.

Additionally, my second cousin Helen Scheurmann-Wild, whose home is in Zürich, Switzerland, has been of invaluable help with the dialect. She has worked diligently to assist with other details, understanding my desires to set my memories in print.

I am indebted to Steve Dzina, a grade school teacher very familiar with children's books, to high school English teacher Andrew Boone for his corrections, and to high school student Austin Retzlaff for his suggestions.

My daughter Claire Naundorf Streb has been very helpful in the technical aspects toward publication as well as final editing and submission. My friend Andrew Beery willingly shared his friendship and computer skills (not to mention the computer itself), and my friends Michael and Jeanne Reagan also helped immeasurably with my computer struggles. My tutor Nitra Hillyer, from the Canandaigua, N.Y. Wood Library, gave me "over-and-above" help in getting me familiar with e-mail so I can communicate with my publisher and others.

My late daughter Geryll Naundorf Norriss, who had lost her sight, was of great support as I read parts of this book to her. She contributed excellent comments to Chapter Twelve. Since she had been an avid reader, she would have been very happy to see this book in print.

The ongoing encouragement of my now late husband Charles H. Naundorf III kept my goal always ahead of me. He often made the difference between an ordinary day and one of greater accomplishment. For example, as an engineer-physicist, he described the working of the locomotive to me, enabling me to write about it knowledgeably. He also carried props and played a tape of Alpine music at appropriate times during my delivery of *Interweaving the Generations,* my one-woman play which was the basis for **The Stories of Emmy.**

Mary Pratt, my editor, helped me polish the manuscript into the finished book you hold in your hands.

Judi Cermak, a retired Bloomfield, N.Y. art teacher and well-known Canandaigua artist, painted the picture of Emmy that is on the front cover of this book. Judi also sketched the Edelweiss flower that precedes each chapter of *The Stories of Emmy.*

I feel blessed in sharing my dream as I bring my very modest mother's anecdotes to you.

DSN

Chapter One

Emmy Picks Flowers

The new morning sun pulled Emmy to the window. She leaned down on her elbows and poked her little red-haired head out as far as she dared. Up the street near the village watering trough, she could see the last of the school-children straggling toward the schoolhouse.

Everywhere up and down Main Street, Emmy could see the sheets and feather-filled comforters the housewives had already piled over windowsills for their airing. Farmer *Schäfer's* cows were drinking at the trough, while the farmer and another villager stopped to talk about the good spring weather. Emmy breathed deeply of the fresh mountain air and felt so happy that summer would soon be here.

The Village of Muttenz

Satisfied with what she had seen outside, Emmy stood and pulled the window down. She went back to getting dressed. First she put on her undergarments and her heavy stockings. Then she sat on the floor and pulled on her sturdy shoes. She was very happy she could lace them all the way up and tie the laces into strong, tight bows. Everyone said she was smart for a five-year-old girl. Last she wiggled into her dress and started down the stairs carrying her hairbrush.

When she entered the bakery store, she found the first customers already chatting with her mother. "*Luise,*" one of the women was saying, "are you feeling well now?"

"*Jo, jo,* I am quite strong, *Frau Frey.*" Then seeing Emmy, they both greeted her. Emmy curtsied politely and wished Mrs. *Frey* a good morning. The woman smiled at the little girl as she and the other customer watched the child's jumble of red curls fall neatly into place as her mother gently brushed them. When her mother was finished, she said, "You may be excused now, Emmy. Hot chocolate and raisin buns are in by *Vatti*."

Emmy walked back through the hallway to the bakery workroom where wonderful smells still hung in the air. Emmy greeted her father with a cheerful "*Guete Daag, Vatti.*" The usually solemn man, who was kneading and punching the dough, smiled at Emmy. *Jakob's* blue, blue eyes twinkled as he watched his youngest daughter munching a raisin bun and drinking her chocolate. He asked if she had completed her chores. When Emmy said she had, her father told her she could run and play.

Emmy really didn't feel like playing with anyone just then. She returned to the bakery store where her mother was now taking a rest on a stool behind the counter. Emmy wandered to the doorway and looked out.

Their village of *Muttenz* — villagers called it "*Muttets*" — seemed to be more awake. Whichever direction she looked, Emmy saw neighbors busy with something. Some women had already pulled in their sheets and feather-filled comforters to make their beds. Others swept their doorsteps. A couple of young mothers pushed babies in tan wicker baby buggies. Here and there a dog or a cat darted across the street. A man guided his horse and wagon around the cows drinking at the trough, and a *Brieffdrääger* — letter carrier — began his rounds of delivering letters.

Konsumerverein ... Consumer Co-op, Muttenz

This same activity was going on all around Switzerland where Emmy and her family lived. Everywhere the streets were neat and clean.

Emmy then saw their next customer, *Frau Tschudin*, coming toward the store. They waved at each other. Emmy turned and said, "Here comes *Frau Tschudi*," and then walked to her mother. "*Mutti*," she asked, "may I go for a walk to the big meadow to pick some flowers?"

Her mother smiled and patted her head. "*Jo, de kasch go, aber de muesch zèèrscht no bim Grossmutti verbyy.*" So, after briefly greeting *Mrs.Tschudin*, Emmy went skipping down the street, singing to herself, "*Mutti* told me I could go. *Mutti* told me I could go, but first I must go to *Grossmutti's* house."

Emmy turned the corner, and as she came near her grandma's house, there was *Grossmutti Sekunda* in the front garden. She was wearing her apron with the big pockets in which she carried her scissors and trowel to help her as she worked among the new lettuce and tomato plants. On either side of the path the new geranium plants lined the way to her door. On the far side, away from where she stood, were the nice straight rows of other flowers that soon would be blooming. Near the foundation of her house were the lily-of-the-valley plants that were called *Maieryysli*. The tiny white flowers that lined the top of the stems really did look like many little bells. Emmy usually sang a song about them with her grandmother, but today Emmy was too excited.

She was so excited that she could hardly speak. She began, "*Guete Morge, Grossmutti*," who answered, "Why, good morning to you, too, Emmy."

Emmy continued, "*Grossmutti*, will you go with me to the meadow to pick flowers?"

Her grandmother smiled, patted Emmy's head, and answered, "Why, of course, little one, I would be glad to do that." She walked across her small front yard and opened the gate on the wrought iron fence in front of her home. The two of them started hand in hand down the street. Before long, Emmy started skipping again.

Then she saw the letter carrier. She ran up to him and said, "*Griessi, Hèèr Brieffdrääger, Grossmutti* and I are going to pick flowers." He, too, patted Emmy's head. "Greetings to you, too," he replied as he nodded at the grandmother.

Emmy and her grandmother walked together to the edge of the village, and finally they reached the meadow. It was filled with all kinds of wild flowers. At first Emmy ran from one place to another. Because they were all so beautiful, she wanted to pick them all at once.

Suddenly, Emmy stopped running and laughed right out loud. "I must look funny," she said to her grandmother. "Guess what! I'm acting just like I do when there is a dish of chocolates and I want to eat them all at once. It's so hard to choose."

So her grandmother helped her get started. "Maybe it will be easier if you begin with one color at a time," she suggested. "I'll show you how." She handed Emmy her garden scissors, and Emmy picked first the yellow flowers, then the blue, and then the smiling white and yellow daisies. It was so much fun. The sun shone down upon them as the butterflies fluttered among the flowers. The old woman and the young child felt so happy together in the countryside. Even the birds singing in the nearby trees sounded especially cheerful.

Emmy's bunch of flowers grew so big she had to give some to her grandmother to hold. Then she turned back to pick some more. Soon, as Emmy's hands became full again, Grandma suggested they start for home. They walked along the side of the country road talking about how pretty the flowers would look in the middle of Mutti's kitchen table. Suddenly Emmy realized that she heard a strange sound. "Brum, brum, bouncety-bounce. Brum, brum, bouncety-bounce."

Emmy turned her head and then . . . she turned all the way around. What was this big black thing that was coming along? It looked like a big, black wagon, but no horse was pulling it!

As Emmy stood there, wide-eyed and wondering, this noisy, bouncy wagon stopped right in front of her and Grandma. It became very quiet. As they watched, a man stepped down from the wagon. He had on a special suit and a special hat to let everyone know he was the driver. Emmy knew it was called a uniform because it looked something like the suit the letter carrier wore. That was special enough, but even more interesting to Emmy was that this man had very, very dark, almost black, skin. Emmy had never seen a black man before, so she stared very hard until she remembered that Mutti had told her it was not polite to stare.

The man tipped his hat to the grandmother, and turning to Emmy, he said in German, "Little girl, the rich woman in the back of this touring car wants me to buy your flowers.

So I have some coins for you, if you will give me those most beautiful flowers."

Emmy looked at her grandmother who smiled and nodded her head. So Emmy stretched out her hand, and the driver took the flowers and gave her the coins. He reached into the touring car, which was a car that was open instead of having windows, and gave the flowers to the woman in the back seat. She leaned forward and waved at them. The driver walked to the front of the car. He bent over and turned a big handle, which started the noisy engine, and then he got back into the car. The woman turned, and looking out through the rear window, waved at the little freckled girl with the high-top shoes and the long dress that almost reached her ankles. The woman, who wore a navy blue straw hat decorated with a veil and artificial flowers, also waved at the grandmother who was wearing her garden apron. The two women also smiled at each other as though they were saying, "Thank you" to each other.

"Brum, brum, bouncety-bounce," they drove down the road away from Emmy and her grandmother who stood watching. When the two people in the touring car were almost out of sight, Emmy and Grandma saw the woman raise her hand again. They returned the wave. Then the touring car was gone.

Emmy was so excited. She had many questions. "*Grossmuetter*," she asked, "What is that black wagon without a horse called? Why does it make so much noise? Why did that lady want my flowers?"

So the grandmother explained that very rich people owned this new kind of vehicle. "The man called it a touring car. It's named '*Auti.*' It has a machine inside that makes it go without a horse." She paused and thought for a moment. "Emmy," her grandmother continued, "I think they wanted to see up close a nice little Swiss girl who looks like Heidi."

"Oh!" replied Emmy. "Why is that man so dark he is almost *schwaarz?*" To this question, her grandmother answered, "Well, Emmy, he is almost black because he came from a faraway place called Africa, and there, it is very hot. Almost everyone has dark skin. You see, this is a very big world we live in and there are all kinds of people in it."

"Oh," said Emmy, and she looked at the coins she held so tightly in her hand. When they got to the grandmother's house, Grandma handed Emmy some of the flowers she had carried for Emmy and gave Emmy a kiss.

Emmy waved goodbye to her grandmother as she went around the corner and ran up the block as fast as the wind. Emmy was huffing and puffing as she reached her home. She called, "*Mutti, Mutti*, guess what! Guess what!" The words tumbled out of Emmy all at once in one great big long breath: "I had a nice bunch of flowers and then this big black *Auti* came along and a man, a black man, got out and he gave me money for the flowers and then he drove away in the *Auti* and the rich woman in the back waved at me."

Her mother laughed. "Take a breath, dear child, take a breath!"

Everyone in Emmy's family was very excited. At dinner that evening Mutti exclaimed, "Imagine someone with enough money to buy flowers from a little girl!" The family nodded approval. Emmy smiled a big smile. She felt very important.

Chapter Two

Emmy's World Begins to Widen

The day dawned with another beautiful day for Emmy and everyone in her village. Her father and mother were already working downstairs in the bakery. Her sisters had gone on to school. Emmy washed and dressed. Then she ran downstairs where she found her mother again chatting with *Frau Tschudin*, who had come to buy her family's bread.

As she did every morning, Emmy curtsied to the customer and said, "Good morning." Then she excused herself to go into the workroom where raisin buns and hot chocolate awaited her.

"*Guete Daag, Vatti*," she greeted her father who was mixing a huge bowl of batter that he would make into cupcakes. He looked up and smiled at his youngest girl for whom he usually also had a twinkle in his blue eyes.

"*Also,*" he responded, "*was hesch hütte vor*? It will seem dull after your exciting flower picking adventure yesterday."

His daughter put down her cup in the sink. Then she came over and leaned against the end of the very large wooden bin where Papa kept flour. "*Vatti*, you asked what I'm up to today. I don't need exciting things every day. I can think of my day with *Grossmutti* all the time."

"*Jo, das kasch mache*," her father replied. "No one can take your dreams from you. Now, if your chores are done, you may run and play. Remember, *"Zèèrscht duet me schaffe und noochhäär spiile."*

Emmy nodded to let Papa know she heard him. He had said, "Work comes first and afterward playing."

Their father didn't talk much to his children, but when he did, he often gave them a lesson in good values. As a Swiss he was industrious and lived by strict rules.

So Emmy returned to the front of the building where Mutti worked in the bakery store. Her mother said, "Emmy, I have something to show you." As she bent over to get it, Emmy walked over to her. She stretched her little neck to see what her mother was reaching for. Mutti smiled at Emmy. Then she placed a photograph on the counter.

Jacob Lüscher is standing behind his family,
at his right is their eldest daughter Louise,
his wife Luise Gysin Lüscher holding their
baby Frieda on her lap, at her left is Sophie Elise,
and seated in front of Louise is Marie

Emmy was just tall enough to see it. Mutti sat on her stool and bent her head down a little. They made a special picture, themselves, as their heads with the matching red hair looked downward to study the faces of the parents and their four daughters in the photograph.

With a puzzled look, the five-year-old child turned her face toward her mother's. "Why isn't anyone smiling?" she asked.

Emmy had noticed that no one in this handsome family smiled up at them. Her mother explained, "We cannot smile when we have our pictures taken because we have to remain very still for a long time." Cameras and film moved slowly in the early 1900s.

Emmy's blue eyes brightened with understanding. Her red curls danced as she shook her head. "Oh!" she answered. Then she asked, "Does it hurt to have your picture taken?"

Mutti laughed. *"Werum? Näi näi, Spätzli.* Why? No, no, sweetie. It does feel longer than it really is. It's just that no one can fidget or talk or move after the photographer has everyone posed just right." Then she gave Emmy a brief description of what to expect.

About one hundred years later, it helps us to know that the photographer's movements were much as they are now in the 21st century. He walked behind the camera and looked through the lens at the scene he was about to photograph. There was no button to press. Because of slower film, he had to take the cap off the camera lens to take a "time exposure." The photographer removed the lens cap as he looked at everyone and ordered, "Hold still!" He counted several seconds and put the lens cap back on. Next he asked everyone to stay as they were. Again he called out, "Hold still!" Then he took the cap off again and took another picture. Afterward everyone could move as usual.

Emmy wasn't sure she understood it all, but she responded, "Oh, *Mutti,* when I have my photo taken, I will sit very still." Then she pointed at each person as she said the names. "This man is *Vatti*, and this lady is you." Emmy's mother shook her head and smiled.

Emmy's finger rested on the girl standing next to her father. "Here is my biggest sister Louise." Moving down to the girl sitting on the chair, Emmy pointed out Marie who was holding a magazine. The baby sitting on her mother's lap was Frieda, who was called *Friedi*. Finally, Emmy's finger stopped at the girl who leaned on her mother's arm and shoulder. "This is our sister *Söffi* who is almost as old as Louise."

Emmy continued to study the photo. She exclaimed, "Look, *Mutti*! They all have the same dress on!"

Her mother nodded. She said, "Emmy, I think it looks nice to see all the sisters wearing the same dresses. It makes us look like a real family. It took me a long time to put all those rows of braid on the big collars and long, wide skirts."

Then pointing at her own high-necked dress with its skirt that hung all the way down to the floor, Luise continued. "I made my dress, too, and I sewed *Vatti's* vest and jacket. We looked like such a fine family when we went to the big city to have our pictures taken."

Suddenly Emmy was feeling left out. She asked, "But, *Mutti*, why am I not on the photo? Where am I?"

Emmy's mother smiled as she looked at her little daughter. "Dear little Emmy, you weren't born yet when we went to *Basel* to have this picture taken."

"Oh," the little girl replied as her puzzled look turned happy again. "I will wear my Sunday dress, and you will brush and comb my hair very carefully. When I sit before the man and his camera, I will sit very still. I will not smile either — just like you in this photo."

They turned their faces again toward the photo on the counter. Standing behind his family was *Johann Jakob Lüscher*, who was a very serious Swiss man. He was a baker who owned his very own shop in the village of *Muttenz bi Basel*. About one hundred years later, it is a small modern city not far from the big city of Basel, Switzerland. Although today *Muttenz* is modern, following the custom and culture of that country, the Swiss have kept many of the houses with steep roofs for much more than three hundred years. They are the very same ones that Emmy and her family lived in and saw every day.

Jacob, as we will call him, expected his whole family to help him get the bread and rolls, cinnamon-raisin buns, pies and cakes ready each day for those who came to the store. Jacob wanted no one left out. The two older girls had to carry bags of baked goods to those who couldn't leave their homes — the mothers with tiny babies and the old folks who could not walk far. Jacob wanted everything in good order.

Just as though to remind them, they heard two knocks on the ceiling of the workroom behind them. *"Dr Vatter hed klopft,"* the mother said as she reached for the photo. Emmy's hand stretched out to take the photo so she still could study it.

"Emmy, when *Vatti* knocks on the ceiling with the broom handle, you know he wants me to come to him."

"But we aren't finished, *Mutti*." Emmy put her hand on her mother's arm and begged, "Just another minute, pleeease."

Luise was a pleasant lady. She smiled often and made little jokes with her children. "Just another minute," she answered, as she rose from the stool. She limped to the doorway and called to her husband that she was coming, then turned and told Emmy they would have to put the picture away.

After that was done, Luise limped into the workroom and took the milk pitcher from the shelf, since the knock had reminded her that soon it would be time for lunch. She then moved slowly to the stairs. Emmy watched her with sadness. She knew her mother's legs hurt her. When she walked, she moved with a limp. No one could help to fix them. The doctor didn't know how. He just said, "Put a little salve on your legs and wrap them carefully with bandages. Don't stand up too long."

So Emmy ran to the stairs, carrying a loaf of dark-crusted Swiss white bread upstairs. Her mother climbed slowly up the steps one at a time as a toddler would do.

"Come on, *Mutti*," Emmy said. "*Vatti* will be getting nervous."

"Yes, Emmy, I know. I'm hurrying as fast as I can." As Emmy reached the top, they heard Jacob banging the handle of the broom on the ceiling again. "See, *Mutti*, I told you," Emmy said to her mother.

Luise looked at her child and sighed. "Yes, Emmy, I know you did." She said no more, but she thought to herself, "I will not scold Emmy and say <u>she</u> was the one who wanted extra minutes. She is only a child, and she doesn't know about the grownup world."

Finally Luise reached the top of the stairs, and carrying the milk pitcher, she went into the kitchen to make coffee. Then she sliced the bread and spread butter on each slice. She took a large chunk of Swiss cheese — the kind with the holes — and cut it into smaller pieces. Next she washed and sliced apples to go with the bread and cheese. When the tray of food and coffee was ready, she took the handle from the lid of the stove. Bending over, she knocked twice on the floor to let Jacob know they would soon be carrying it into the baking room.

Emmy went ahead of her mother, carrying the tray of food before her. This time she went down the stairs slowly and carefully. Luise, taking the same step-by-step way of moving on the stairs as she had on her way up, descended. Going down, she could manage the hot pot of coffee without too much trouble. And before long, the mother and child had brought the family's lunch into the bakery workroom.

Jacob and Luise sat on top of barrels containing sugar. Each had a large metal lid on it to cover the sugar. His tiredness was from being up since early morning, lifting and bending. Hers was from waiting on customers and going up and down stairs.

Jacob looked at Luise and quietly asked, "Did you talk to her yet?"

"*Jo*," Luise responded. "She understands."

"Good!" Then looking at Emmy, Jacob asked, "Well, are you ready to go to the photographer tomorrow?"

Emmy's eyes widened. "Tomorrow? Tomorrow?" she asked.

"Yes, tomorrow is the day. Tomorrow there is no school. So *Luggi und Söffi* will take care of the bakery. Your mother and you and I will go together on the train into the city."

"Oh!" answered Emmy who looked like she had just seen the cow jump over the moon. She could hardly believe it. Not only would she wear her Sunday dress on a day that wasn't Sunday, but she would ride on a train, and she would sit very still on a chair in a photographer's shop. She wouldn't even smile.

Just then the front bakery door banged open. Emmy ran to tell her sisters she would be going to the photographer's the next day. Sophie, who was always fast, was first inside. She hardly listened. She burst into the workroom and exclaimed, "I am so mad at that fresh boy!"

Her father calmly asked, "Which one is that?"

Sophie's face was so flushed it was almost as red as her hair. Her face grew redder. "Who is it? Of course, it is *Günther Ruedi*! Who else pulls on my pigtails and stares at my freckles and calls me Copper Face because of these terrible brown dots?" Her voice raised higher and louder, "Who else?"

"Yes, I know it is not pleasant to be made fun of," her mother said to Sophie. "I didn't like it very much either. But you must not get so excited, *Söffi*. The boys do that to the girls because they like them. The more you get angry, the more they will do it."

"But I hate him," Sophie replied. "I just want to smack his face!"

"Enough of this nonsense," Jacob told his daughter. "Boys always tease girls when they're your age. Your mother is right. If they didn't like you, they would ignore you. Now! Be quiet and eat your lunch or you will be late for school."

Sophie hung her head and slowly began to munch on her bread and cheese. She said no more words, but it was easy to see that was not the end of her anger at *Günther Ruedi*.

In the meantime, Louise had come in. Her forehead glistened with perspiration. "May I have a glass of water, please?" she asked. "It is so warm out there. I wish we didn't have to wear these heavy stockings when it's almost summertime."

Fearing another outburst of an excitable teenager, Mutti told her to sit quietly and eat her food and drink her milk. Then Mutti took a cloth and dampened it with a small amount of water. "Here, *Luggi*, wipe your face with this. When you are finished, I will brush your hair for you and make a new ponytail."

"Thank you, *Mutti*," answered Louise. She was the eldest daughter. She knew it was best to remain calm.

No sooner had that been settled, when Frieda and Marie, the blonde ones, walked in. As usual, Marie was carrying a book. She was walking and reading at the same time. No one in the family could ever remember when Marie had not been reading. In fact, her parents sometimes joked that she had come into the world holding a book. It was not easy for anyone to become annoyed with her or to scold her. Marie was a sweet girl who lived in another world.

Where Marie was, Frieda was not far behind. Emmy looked at her sister and thought, "*Friedi* doesn't talk very much, but she can do anything. People don't think she is smart because she is so quiet. They don't know."

The two girls said that school was fine and quietly ate their lunch. Their father shook his head with satisfaction to know that they would be girls he could trust with his bakery. He was pleased with his decision that when he was gone the next day, all of them would be in charge of the bakery store. He announced, "*Luggi* can do the baking, and *Söffi* can run the errands as she usually does. *Friedi* and Marie will wait on customers."

Emmy watched and listened. She wasn't sure which she liked better, when she was at home alone or when her sisters were home from school. It was more interesting when they were there. Yet, when she was alone, things went smoother.

She looked at Marie and Frieda and said very quietly, "Tomorrow I'm going to the photographer's in Basel with *Mutti* and *Vatti*. I will sit very still."

Frieda and Marie gave Emmy a hug before they said, "Good-bye," and started back to school for the afternoon. Louise and Sophie started soon afterward. Then it was quiet again.

Emmy was out in the store again with her mother. "*Mutti*, "Emmy said, "*Vatti* told me to go play. May I go to play with *Elise*?"

"All right," *Mutti* agreed. "Just don't stay very long." Emmy kissed her mother and scampered out the door. Her head spun with her thoughts as she ran down the street. When she reached her friend Elise's house, Emmy called to her. "Elise, I can play a little while. Let's jump rope." As Elise went to get her rope, Emmy called, "Guess what! I'm going to the photographer's tomorrow!"

Chapter Three

Emmy Travels to the Big City

Yesterday Emmy had learned she was going to the photographer's studio on Saturday. Her mother awakened
her and called her to a breakfast of oatmeal. When Emmy
finished eating, her mother took a pan of warm water, soap,
a cloth and towel into the bedroom Emmy shared with Marie
and Frieda.

After instructing Emmy to do a good thorough job of
cleaning herself, Mutti laid out Emmy's best Sunday clothes.
Then she went into her own room to begin dressing for their
trip to Basel.

Coming up from the bakery workroom, *Vatti* poured himself a pan of water from a kettle that had been heating on the
stove. He too set about scrubbing himself for their day out.
Next, he took a hand mirror and set it down near the kitchen
window where he stood and trimmed his moustache almost
as carefully as he designed flowers on a wedding cake.

Just as Jacob was finished, Luise came into the room and
asked him to help her button her dress. As he struggled with
the small buttons, Jacob confided to his wife that he would

be grateful for the rest from his work. "I hope you will be, too, Luise. It will be a nice outing for the three of us."

He then added, "I feel very satisfied that *Luggi* will do good work today while we are gone. I have explained all the recipes and duties with her. She is a bright girl and a hard worker."

Luise nodded and smiled. Louise, being the eldest, naturally had been taught a strong sense of responsibility. In those days, before many labor-saving appliances, it was common for businessmen to have young teenage children working for them. In this case, Louise would be given the task of taking her father's place as the baker, whom she had watched and helped many times.

As she walked to the bedroom where Emmy was dressing, Jacob watched his wife. He smiled to himself and thought, "Also, I have selected a fine looking woman to be *Luggi's* mother."

Luise Gysin Lüscher, Emmy's mother

Luise found Emmy almost dressed. She was excitedly chatting to her sisters about the day that lay ahead. They, in turn, were happy for her, but Frieda could hardly keep her eyes open. "She always is a sleepyhead," Emmy thought as she went into the kitchen to join her father. Soon afterward Mutti, too, came from giving Marie and Frieda last-minute instructions. Then the parents and their youngest daughter went downstairs, said "*Wiiderluege*" to Louise and Sophie, and walked out the door.

There, Farmer *Schäfer* had just pulled up with his simple farm wagon, and jumped down to help Luise climb into the front where she could sit on the seat next to him. Behind him, he had placed two milking stools where Jacob and Emmy sat with their backs up against the farmer's seat. It would not be a fancy ride to the *Yysebaan* — the Train Station — but they would get there on time.

Driving the several blocks to the train station, Emmy excitedly chattered to her father. "Will we get there in time, *Vatti*?" she asked. "*Mutti* says we must be there early, so we will not miss the train."

"*Jo, jo*," replied her father. "In a country that makes such fine watches and clocks, of course the *Zùùg* runs on time. It is up to the passengers to be there early so the conductors can keep their schedule."

"The *Zùùg*, the train, is never late?"

"Of course not! We Swiss cannot even imagine such a thing!" her father assured Emmy.

By then, Farmer *Schäfer's* fine horse came to the station and the farmer pulled on the reins. "Here we are," he announced to his passengers. He jumped down from the seat, and went around to the other side to help Luise down, while Jacob hopped out and reached his arms up to lift Emmy down to the ground. "*Danggerschehen, Willi*, thank you!" Jacob said to the farmer. "I told Marie and *Friedi* not to charge you for your pie and bread today."

31

The farmer smiled and nodded. He gave Jacob a pat on the back, and replied, "Well, that was not necessary. What are friends for? But since you told the girls, I thank you very much. I'll be back this evening to meet you." Giving a wave to the three travelers, he climbed back into his wagon and returned in the direction of the village and his farm.

Then the baker, his wife and their daughter walked to the train station. On the platform outside the small building, Jacob and Luise nodded to a number of their regular customers who had also assembled for the train ride into Basel. Emmy and her mother stood to one side while Jacob walked to the window to purchase three tickets.

Everyone watched. This was a natural thing. The most recent arrivals anywhere usually draw the attention of those who are already waiting. There was special attention, however, when the *Lüschers* arrived. One woman, putting her hand to her lips to keep her words private, said to her husband. "I wonder who died. *Lüscher* Jacob never takes his family anywhere. I wonder why they are taking only Emmy."

Her husband, not politely quiet as his wife, answered, "It can't be a death, *Hildi*. Then all the family would go. I heard him telling someone at church last week he was leaving his girls to run the bakery today."

"Is that so? And you didn't tell me?" The wife looked annoyed as though she had missed out on the most important gossip the village had heard in weeks. The husband rolled his eyes and said, "Be quiet, *Hildi*, here they come."

Turning to the *Lüscher* family, he smiled and heartily greeted the man, "*Guete Daag, Jakob*. We see your *frau* and *dòchter* — wife and daughter — are with you. Are you visiting someone in Basel today? Is someone ill?"

Behind him, his wife smiled as though Luise was her dearest friend. She nodded and waited to hear the reason for this unusual trip for the baker and his wife.

"Oh, no," Jacob replied. "No one is sick. We are taking Emmy to have her photo taken at the studio."

Hildi, the man's wife, couldn't believe her ears. The baker had a reputation for being very frugal. She couldn't believe he would spend the money for such an unnecessary thing as a photograph of their daughter. The words burst from her mouth, "You are spending the money for that?" Her husband looked at her with a frown.

Luise stiffened. She was not sure what her husband would reply. She was relieved to see Jacob smile as he replied, "But, of course! It isn't everyone who has such a beautiful child. She wasn't with us yet when the rest of the family had our photos taken, so we are making a special trip just for her."

The other onlookers smiled, too. It wasn't every day that the town gossip had someone answer so nicely to her thoughtless words. They had to hand it to Jacob. He was the most honest and polite man they knew. He had a good wife and five wholesome daughters.

Before anyone else could say a word, the train entered the station. The steam engine was puffing smoke and gushing steam, but just like everything else in their little country, the outside of the engine and the passenger cars were shiny and bright. Not only did the trains run on time, they looked very nice, as well.

The conductor helped the women step up onto the train. He nodded to the men. He didn't say anything to the children who, in those days, were to be seen and not heard. Emmy sat closest to the window. Her mother and father sat alongside her calm and quiet, like all good Swiss were expected to do.

The conductor, still standing on the ground, signaled the engineer to start. The engine chugged. All who had watches, looked at them and nodded with satisfaction. They departed just on time, and soon would be in Basel.

When they disembarked, Jacob looked around for a carriage to take them to the photographer's studio. It was perhaps a mile or so from the railroad station. So, although he hated to spend the money, he hired the carriage to take them along *Aeschevorstadt* and *Freii Strooss* past the many shops in the city. Because it was an open carriage, Emmy was able to look around as though her head was on a swivel. Everywhere were people. People in carriages like theirs, people walking, people standing, people entering stores.

As they continued on toward the Rhine River, they reached the bridge called *Mittleri Brugg.* Emmy was very excited to see the large river. Never had she seen anything like it. The streams she had seen near their home were tiny in comparison. She found it exciting to see the many different sights.

Having crossed the bridge, they now passed a street called *Gryyffegass* and continued on a short distance when the driver turned his head and announced, *"Clarastrooss fümf."* Then he drew up in front of Five Clara Street. They were just in time for their appointment. After handing the driver some coins, Jacob led Emmy and Luise to the studio.

Emmy stared through the clear, clean glass at the beautiful display inside the window. A heavy dark red curtain hung across the top and down on either side. Carefully arranged were several photographs of elegant people looking out at Emmy and her parents.

The door opened, and *Herr Carl Schmid,* the photographer, stepped toward them and said, *"Willkùmme!* Welcome! You must be *Herr* and *Frau Lüscher.* Come in." Then turning to Emmy, he smiled and added, "And this must be Emmy." The three nodded, and followed him into his studio.

The man, whose sandy hair was longer than her father's dark hair, was a few years younger than he was, too. Mr. *Schmid* continued to smile, and as he clasped his hands lightly near his waist, he bowed slightly toward them. Emmy had never seen anyone so polite to her parents. "So, you already have a photo of your whole family. Now, since you have this new little girl, you want a photo taken of her. Is this right?"

Emmy's father, looking as though he enjoyed the special attention, agreed the man was correct. Mr. *Schmid* smiled some more and indicated two chairs. "Please have a seat here. Let's see what we can do to take a photo to make you proud of your daughter."

He bent even farther down, and said in his smooth, quiet voice, "Emmy, please come with me." Emmy was not sure how to act, so she looked at her parents for permission to follow. They nodded their heads. She followed the photographer. She decided she liked him. He treated her like a grown up person.

When the photographer had taken her a few feet across the room, he said, "Let's put you up on this chair." Putting his hands under her arms, he lifted the little five-year-old girl and placed her on the chair. He stood up and stepped back. Satisfied that the child's gingham dress looked just right, he said, "Here is a photo for you to hold." Then he walked behind his camera, just as Emmy's mother had told Emmy he would.

Emmy, A Girl Like Heidi

Mr. *Schmid* came out from behind the camera and started to explain to Emmy what he would do. This time it was Emmy's turn to nod. She bobbed her head up and down to let him know she understood. "Good!" he said. "I can see you know what to expect. Your mother did a good job getting you ready. Now, do you know you cannot move or blink while I'm taking your photo?"

"Oh, yes, sir," Emmy answered. "*Mutti* says I must not move at all. I will sit very still."

The photographer replied, "Yes, you are right. This big black box is my camera. It has a lens that acts like an eye. It has a cap that is something like an eyelid that is closed." Pointing to it, he continued, "I will go behind the camera, and I'll put my head under the cloth. I will reach in front of the camera and remove the cap just as though I'm opening the camera's eye. You must sit very still until I replace the cap in front of the lens and I come out."

And that's just what Emmy did two times. She didn't move, and she didn't smile, exactly as she had promised.

"Very good," the photographer said as he lifted Emmy down. When she and her parents were all standing together, Mr. *Schmid* explained, "This will take a few days, *Herr Lüscher*. I will prepare the photos and put them in fine cardboard frames like these on the counter. If you will pay me now, I will send the photos through the postal system."

Jacob thanked the man and paid for the work. He then asked if there was a bakery or tearoom nearby. The little family left as the photographer called, "*Uff Wiiderluege,*" after them.

Walking down the block, as the photographer had suggested, Jacob soon found the bakery. "Come in with me," he said to Emmy and her mother. They entered and sat at a small table, while Jacob went to the glass case and selected pastries and hot chocolate for the three of them. When he, too, sat at the table and had passed around the sweet rolls and chocolate, Jacob picked up his pastry and smelled it. "It smells pretty good," he announced, "but I can do better. They could have used a little more butter, I think. Someday, I shall have a bakery in the city."

Luise and Emmy had heard him mention his dream many times, so they nodded politely while they enjoyed the drink and food. Emmy was more interested in watching people as they came in and out of the store. She also noticed that the young woman, who served the customers from behind the counter, as her mother did at home, was wearing a kerchief on her head. She would ask *Mutti* about that later.

Her mother, meanwhile, noticed the clothing the people wore and mentally planned how she would sew the next dresses she'd make for her daughters. Emmy's father was by then looking out onto the street where many carriages carried passengers as other people walked along past the bakery shop.

"Luise," he announced, "as soon as we are ready, we can take a carriage across the new bridge, *Wettschtaibrugg.* Emmy will enjoy seeing the river again. Then we can turn to go to *Munschterplatz* where the cathedral is located. This is where our Great Reformers preached. It is a splendid building." Noticing that they were now ready, he added, "Come along, then."

Riding in the carriage was fun for Emmy. Her hair blew around as they passed over small boats carrying people of all kinds. On the other side, she saw children, big and small, walking with their parents. Suddenly she said excitedly, "Look! Look! There is a black man just like *Grossmutti* and I saw when we were picking flowers. I wonder if he is the man who gave me the coins."

Her parents smiled, seeing that their little girl was happy to see life in the city. "He might be the same man," Mutti answered. "He does have on a uniform. We do not see many dark people in our land. It is hard to tell from here."

Emmy nodded, and as though thinking, replied, "M-m-m-m." She hoped it was because he had been very nice to her. Suddenly remembering her question, she asked Mutti, "Why did the girl in the bakery wear a kerchief on her head?"

Mutti was unsure. She looked for the answer from Vatti who replied, "There is a rule in the city that all people who work with food must cover their heads to keep stray hairs from falling into the food. It is a new idea that we in the villages will have to follow after awhile."

"Thank you, *Vatti*," said Emmy, whose attention was once again on the surrounding city streets. There seemed to be more wagons and carriages crowding the street, and there was a greater number of people moving on foot. When they reached the cathedral, they left the carriage and stood at the metal railing to watch the passengers on boats in the water. The sun was warm. Everyone seemed to be having a good time.

Jacob looked at his watch and announced they had better walk over to the cathedral if they were going to get to the train on time. And as they walked toward the beautiful large church, Emmy drew in her breath. "Oh!" she said. She stared and stared. It was made of brownish-red brick and its steeples were much, much higher and more decorated than the one on their small Saint *Arbogast* Church that Louise had told her was built in the old days of the Holy Roman Empire.

When they reached the wide steps and followed other visitors through the open doorway, Jacob remarked how strong and beautiful the large carved doors were. They went in and stood in the back looking at the beauty of the windows, the polished pews, the lights, and at the front where the communion table with candles was placed. Emmy's eyes were wide at everything she saw. Her father pointed out the special pulpit above the pews where the pastor stood to preach.

Luise sat in a pew to rest. After they had looked around some more and said a prayer, it was time to go. Outside, Emmy's father stopped another carriage, and they all climbed in, after which Jacob gave the driver instructions.

"This time, we will drive down past some houses," he said. As they drove down the side streets, Emmy couldn't believe what she saw. The houses were mostly tan and brown and were often connected to each other. Sometimes they were separated by narrow paths that were called *Gässli*. They represented the proud way Swiss owners had cared for their property through many years. Here and there were bright red geraniums in window boxes. It was a wonderful sight.

Emmy's mother was most fascinated by the beautifully carved wooden doors. These doors had ornate brass handles.

Every few houses they passed, Luise would say, "Jacob, look at that one! How beautiful!" Emmy was so happy to see her mother enjoying herself. When she looked at her father, even he looked pleased. Then he saw a tearoom. "*Halt! Bitti, halt!*" he called to the carriage driver. "Would you please take us back to that tearoom?"

The driver turned and pulled to the side. Jacob paid him and helped Luise and Emmy down to the ground. "Come with me," he said to them. "One last chance to eat in Basel." They entered the tearoom where Jacob asked for sandwiches and coffee, and then he added, "Do you have any *Bääredrägg?*"

Emmy asked, "Licorice, *Vatti*, why licorice?"

"Emmy, we have had a nice day here in Basel. Don't you think your sisters need a treat for all the hard work they are doing while we are here?" her father questioned her.

"Oh, sure," answered Emmy, who hadn't thought of *Muttets* and her sisters all day. Just then the woman brought their food, so they all began eating.

"M-m-m, *d'Wùùrscht* is delicious, and the bread isn't too bad either," Luise ventured to say. Jacob looked a little surprised when his wife expressed her opinion so readily. At the beginning of the 20th century, most women weren't so bold to speak out so openly. Jacob wondered what caused Luise to do so. Then he smiled. "Luise, I haven't smelled the bread. I think I don't have to, if you approve. You have worked together with me long enough in my bakery to know good bread when you taste it."

Then, he took a big bite, and joined his wife and daughter in the delicious lunch. When all three had eaten, Jacob reminded them, "Now, we must move along. It will soon be time to go to the *Yysebahn*."

Soon after, they were back at the train station where they saw some of the neighbors who had traveled with them that morning. Many carried packages from shopping all day.

40

Jacob felt a bit strange with only a package of licorice from a tearoom, but no one seemed really to notice anything except that Basel seemed to have had a good effect on the three *Lüschers*.

Before long, the train pulled into the station and the people lined up to go into the passenger car. Because Luise was tired, she and Jacob and Emmy waited to be last. It was almost time for the train to leave the station, and as Emmy was reaching the conductor, he gave the nod to the engineer. At once the piston began its work and its arm went back and forth to turn the wheel. The smoke puffed and the steam gushed. Emmy was so fascinated watching this happen that she forgot to step up onto the train. The conductor seemed irritated as he signaled to the engineer to stop. Turning to Emmy, he then said, "Hurry, *Maiteli!* Little girl, the train must leave!"

Emmy hurried up the steps and into the car. Everyone stared at her, thinking Emmy was a very bold child to keep the train from leaving on time. Her mother smiled, and patting the seat next to her, said, "Come sit down, Emmy. Trains are very interesting, aren't they?"

"Yes, *Mutti*. You know what I was thinking? I wonder if the touring cars have things like those iron parts that make trains move. That must be what *Grossmutti* meant by a machine that makes the *Auti* go." Jacob, who was of course listening, nodded his head. He told Emmy she had exactly the right idea. Emmy smiled, and shook her head. She felt very good about their trip to Basel.

As they had planned, Mr. *Schäfer* and his trusty horse and wagon were waiting at the *Muttenz* station to take them home. When they reached the bakery, the sisters all asked about their day. And when their father asked how everything went for them, they said, "Fine."

Louise, who was a very outgoing, happy girl, laughed and asked, "Oh, who do you think helped *Söffi* deliver bread and rolls today?" She glanced at Sophie, and before anyone else had a chance to say anything, added, "It was *Günther Ruedi!*"

Sophie's normally bright pink face grew red. She pretended not to hear what Louise had said, but smiled to herself as though she had a big secret. It was embarrassing to her to be the center of the family's smiling attention, yet it made her feel very good at the same time.

Jacob stepped over to her and said, "There is a surprise in this bag for you and your sisters to share. I thank all of you for doing a good job. I'm very proud of you."

The four sisters said, "Thank you, *Vatti*," and willingly took their share of their favorite licorice.

Emmy, who was bursting to tell all about her adventures in the big city, noticed her mother's face. It seemed as though she was telling Emmy, "Not now." So, Emmy knew it was best to be quiet. Her sisters, who had stayed at home in their village, needed a little attention now. Later, Emmy could tell them and her friends all about her exciting day in the big city.

Chapter Four

Emmy Tells the Time at School

Emmy continued to grow after her special trip to the big city of Basel. She learned many things, and finally she was ready to go to school as her sisters did. She walked with them to the one-story stucco building where she would learn to read and write and do arithmetic. She was so happy to see children from the other edge of her village, and she even liked doing what certain grown-ups other than her parents asked her to do. One day, when she was seven years old, *dr Hèèr Lèèrer* caught Emmy's excited attention. He reminded the class how important time was to the Swiss. "After all, children, our country makes the finest timepieces — watches and clocks — in the whole world. So, we must know how to tell time."

Emmy's heart jumped. She, like every other young girl, had the sincere wish to have a beautiful shiny timepiece hanging around her neck. This is what they saw on the lovely women at St. Arbogast Church on Sundays. As their teacher spoke about why it was important to tell time, Emmy dreamed more and more of owning her very own watch on a chain around her neck. Later, she talked about it so much at home that her mother figured out a way for Emmy to have one. "Emmy, it is only a make-believe watch, but it will be fun for you," Mutti told her. Emmy smiled and gave her mother a big hug to thank her.

So, the next morning, Emmy brought her very own watch to school. Well, it wasn't a real watch. It was really a coin with a hole in the center, and it hung around her neck on a long ribbon just like the most expensive Swiss watch hanging on a chain of a grown-up fashionable woman.

Before the classroom door opened, Emmy and her friends were having fun playing the game, *"Was isch für Zyt, Emmy?"* To play the game of "What time is it, Emmy?" a schoolmate would ask her what time it was, and Emmy, after looking at her make-believe watch, would answer. The girls giggled and the boys shoved in for a closer look, and then *Hèèr Schaub* (the teacher) opened the door.

"Guete Morge, Kinder," he said. And when they didn't answer as usual, more loudly his voice called again, "Good morning, children."

This time, several of the laughing children stood at attention and answered, *"Guete Morge, Hèèr Schaub."* Then one by one they walked into the classroom, with Emmy and a couple of boys trailing behind, still playing the game. Emmy's face was rosy red with the attention and excitement. Emmy's red curls bounced as she and the two boys passed their teacher, mumbling, "Good morning, *Hèèr Schaub*," to him as they went to their seats.

They sat in rows of wooden school seats and desks that were hooked onto each other. Their classroom looked very much like the ones we see on television shows about the olden days like "Dr. Quinn, Medicine Woman." At the front of the room was a blackboard, and over to one side, near the door, was a square red flag with a white cross in the middle of it. This was the Swiss flag. In the far corner of the room was a rather tall, boxy metal stove with which the room was heated in the cold weather.

Mr. Schaub had a wooden desk with a lift-up cover on it and long, wooden legs to hold it up. The teacher was a very proper looking man with his hair slicked to his head and tiny wire spectacles perched toward the end of his nose. He wore a dark suit, a white shirt with a very stiff collar and a dark ribbon tie. His shoes laced up above his ankles, just like the ones the *Brieffdrddger* wore when he delivered the mail. The teacher was even more serious than Emmy's father. He frowned as he thought about the strange way the children had acted when he opened the door. Something was not right. He decided to watch and listen very carefully to learn what the problem was. He was not about to have any nonsense in his classroom. The children rose to sing a song that was their promise to love their fatherland, followed by their morning prayer together. When they were seated, the teacher began the roll call. As the roll was being taken, *Fritz* leaned over from the seat behind Emmy and whispered to her, *"Was für Zyt?"* Still in the spirit of the game, Emmy turned her smiling face down to her round make-believe watch, *"Halber nyni.* Half past eight.*"* So engrossed was Emmy in telling the time, she didn't hear the great stillness in the room. When she turned to see why *Fritz* didn't answer her, Emmy saw him looking above her head with a look of fear on his face. She glanced at the other children behind her, and they all sat at attention with the same frightened expression. Turning forward in her seat, Emmy at last saw Mr. Schaub glowering down upon her over the top of his little spectacles.

"Lùscher, Emmy," he thundered, *"Jetz dien mr wiider schaffe!"* As he repeated, "Now we do work again!" the teacher added, "I will have proper behavior in my class-room! This is not playtime!" At this statement, Mr.Schaub snatched the ribbon and coin from around Emmy's neck, and ordered the little girl to put out her hand. The hickory stick whistled through the air as it cracked down across her palm. Smack! Smack! Smack! The stick smarted against the palm of Emmy's hand. Tears welled in her eyes. Her head was bowed, and her heart sank way deep inside her, way back where no one could see. And Emmy thought to herself, "I know I shouldn't have been playing in class, and I'm sorry." Tears rolled down her cheeks. She sniffed and thought, "Now I don't even have my play watch anymore. Some day when I'm grown up, I'll have my very own real watch on a chain around my neck!"

Along with her classmates, Emmy raised her head and continued to learn how to tell the difference between the hour hand and the minute hand. Then she smiled to herself, remembering that the trains always run on time in Switzerland.

Chapter Five

The Circus Comes to Town

It was now summertime. School was out. Windows all around *Muttenz* were open to catch the refreshing breezes. Odors of baking delicacies floated out around the village from the *Lüscher* Bakery.

Suddenly voices of children outside the bakery cried, *"Do kùnnt der Zirkus! Do kùnnt der Zirkus!"* Children came running from all directions, and then the grownups. Even the five *Lüscher* girls were out there. The littlest one, Emmy, with her red curls flying behind her, ran into the bakery store calling, *"Mutti, Mutti,* the circus is coming!" Emmy's mother turned and called, *"Jakob, Jakob,* the circus has come to town. Hurry, Hurry!"

Emmy's father stopped punching and kneading the dough, pulled off his apron, washed his hands, and closed the bakery door behind him. There was hardly a person in the little village of *Muttenz,* Switzerland, who didn't show up for the circus.

It was a very exciting event. The gaily-colored wooden circus wagon drew to a stop, and people spilled into the road. The driver, wearing a herdsman's shirt, rough trousers and

47

an alpine hat, patted his horse. He then grabbed a pail to get water for the faithful animal from the village watering trough. Next the clown, with his gaudy clothes and big, fat, red nose, turned cartwheels. Then the tightrope walkers stepped out, and the musician with his *Handòòrgele* started his act. Last, the dainty singer alighted from the wagon. She was dressed in a traditional Swiss peasant costume. The white cotton blouse had colorful stitching at the neckline and beautiful, bright flowers at the front opening. She wore this with a dark blue full skirt, protected with an apron decorated with embroidered *Edelweiss* alpine flowers. She was truly a lovely sight.

Almost at once the clown was juggling, the musician was playing the small accordion, and the lovely lady was singing her first happy notes. The grownups nodded and smiled to hear the beloved mountain songs. It was, however, when the singer began the wonderful yodeling that the children jumped and laughed and called for more. In the meantime, the tightrope walkers looked for a place to set up their equipment, and got ready to walk and balance themselves across the street.

All eyes eagerly looked up at them. Emmy and her sisters held their breath as *Fraulein Anni* clutched her tightly-closed parasol and took her first shaky step. She seemed to think, "Will I make it this time?" She drew her foot backward onto the platform. She stood still, caught her breath and calmed herself. Then she stepped more bravely onto the rope and made her way to the center, gliding gracefully, like a dancer, along the tightrope. Soon she was near the other side.

Hèèr Hans followed *Anni*. He held his balancing pole and stepped confidently onto the rope. The crowd was very still. They didn't move. Their faces were eager, waiting, waiting for the two people to reach the other side. A very long time seemed to pass. And then a shout burst from everyone. "Bravo! Bravo!" they yelled. The tightrope walkers bowed and smiled, and slid quickly down the pole. Two strong men carried them on their shoulders to the circus wagon, where they sat on the driver's bench like a king and queen, watching the crowd enjoy the sunny afternoon.

It was at this point that Jacob called to his wife and daughters to help him as he hurried to his store. Soon he came out calling, "Cookies for everyone!" Luise and the girls carried large trays of cookies into the crowd, and soon the treats were gone.

The wagon driver passed his hat, and people dropped coins into it to show how much they loved the show. After the crowd thinned and the wagon rumbled out of town, Jacob went back to kneading dough. Luise continued her cleaning while their daughters wandered away with their friends — all except Emmy's sister Frieda. Shy, quiet nine-year-old, blonde-haired Frieda seemed to have something on her mind. In fact, for the next few days she seemed to be in another world. Every day, when her chores were done, Frieda walked around their backyard. Sometimes she looked at the house. Sometimes she examined the railing at the back steps. Frieda definitely seemed to be planning something.

One day, not long after, eight-year-old Emmy saw Frieda carrying their jump rope out into the backyard, so she followed her sister. "What are you doing, *Friedi*?" she asked.

"You'll see," answered Frieda. "Come help me," she continued as she pointed at a place on the step railing where she had poked one end of the rope. "Here, Emmy, pull the end of this rope through, and help me tie a strong, tight knot." The two girls worked together to do a good job. By the time they were finished, Frieda and Emmy had the rope stretched across a corner of the yard and tied to the fence. It wasn't high like the circus tightrope. It was only as high as their knees, but it was off the ground. Soon Frieda was ready to walk across. She climbed up the back steps and reached her foot out onto the rope. She fell and flopped. She slipped and sat on the ground. But Frieda knew she could do it. Emmy helped her. Emmy encouraged her sister. "You can do it!" she told her.

And finally, after lots of practice, Frieda did it. She wiggled and wobbled right across the corner of the backyard! Frieda was ready to begin.

The neighbor kids gathered to watch. "Ladies and gentlemen," shouted Emmy in her very deepest voice. "*Fraulein Friedi* is going to do a death-defying act. Watch her skill. Watch her bravery."

Frieda stepped onto the top step. She swallowed. She put the broom handle in her hands. She took a step, another and then another. Frieda was going to be the village's very own tightrope walker! She was doing very, very well and Emmy knew Frieda would make it. Well . . . she would have, except that the *Seiler's* cat came running around the corner of the house with her body stretched out really long, and her feet carrying her as fast as could be across the backyard, followed by the loudly barking *Müller's* dog.

Startled by the commotion, Frieda fell off the rope. She saw stars when she hit her head. The village kids all laughed. As they ran home, Emmy cried, "Come back, come back! I know she can do it."

But the village kids ran home. Emmy hugged Frieda and said she'd be right back. She ran into the house and soon returned with a glass of cool water. Frieda smiled at her little sister, and together they agreed that tomorrow was another day.

Chapter Six

Emmy Lives at Grossmuetter's House

Emmy certainly loved being with *Grossmuetter Sekunda* and living in her house. Emmy came to live there with her mother and sisters when Jacob *Lüscher* sold his bakery in *Muttenz*, Switzerland, and went away to buy a new bakery in *Amerika*.

The townspeople could hardly believe Jacob *Lüscher* was leaving the bakery and country he loved so much. Jacob's friends knew, though, that he had big plans for a more successful life in a place of greater opportunity. The men slapped his back and shook his hand. They wished him a good trip.

The women told Emmy's mother they knew things would turn out well, and said, "Living at your mother's house will give you a rest, Luise. With your legs hurting so, you can rest." Emmy's mother shook her head and agreed it would be more restful than working in a bakery. The sores on her legs, the ones that the doctors didn't know how to make better, were getting worse. When Emmy's father left, he smiled at all of them and stepped over to the girls. "Behave yourselves and make me proud," he told them. With his wife, he had a few quiet words and a touch on her shoulder. *Vatti* shook the grandmother's hand and said, "Also! Thank you for your help."

Farmer *Schäfer* arrived with his wagon to take Jacob and his belongings to the train station. His family stood with him in a little group, and they all said, *"Wiiderluege*, we'll see you again." He got onto the wagon and they waved to him until he was out of sight. When they could not see him anymore, the five girls and two women went into the grandmother's house and talked about how different everything felt.

After awhile they decided where everyone would sleep and what kind of arrangements they would make for the household chores. *Grossmuetter Sekunda* said, "Luise, this will be a good chance for you to rest your legs, so you will not do much. Maybe sometimes you can give me a hand with the laundry." Louise had helped *Vatti* in the bakery, so she could make the bread, and Sophie was assigned to the shopping and putting her cooking skills to work. Marie and Frieda's jobs were to straighten the rooms. And last, Emmy was asked to do the garden. Emmy loved helping *Grossmuetter Sekunda* in her garden. She found many things to do. Sometimes she pulled weeds. Other times she carried pails of water to *Grossmuetter*. It was such fun being in the bright sun and feeling the warm breeze passing over her skin.

Emmy loved helping her grandmother make *Schänggeli* in her kitchen. *Grossmutti* asked Emmy to stir the eggs and butter together and then add sugar and flour. After the soft, sticky dough was ready, they each took a ball of the dough and rolled it between their fingertips. This way they made something that looked like a buttery sausage or finger. After that, only *Grossmutti* worked at the stove. She melted butter in a deep pan, and slid the "fingers" into the very hot grease.

They smelled so delicious as each piece of the dough turned all brown on the outside. When they were ready, *Grossmutti* dipped in and took each *Schänggeli* out to drain, and later to cool on a clean towel. When they were all finished, the woman poured milk for herself and Emmy. It was then that Emmy could dunk her *Schänggeli* into the milk and bite the crunchy dessert. "M-m-m-m," she and her grandmother said. The crunchy crust and the wonderful golden inside of the *Schänggeli* really tasted good!

When Mutti and all the girls came together for supper and *Schänggeli*, they talked about *Vatti*. The family all agreed they missed him, but living at *Grossmutti's* house was wonderful. Having no chores in the bakery gave them more time to visit with friends or take walks. Emmy even asked her mother one day, "*Mutti*, do you think living at *Grossmuetter's* house is something like being in Heaven?"

Emmy's mother admitted it did feel special. Then a few weeks later, the letter came to call Emmy's sisters Louise and Sophie to help their father save money in *Amerika*. They were now young ladies who had finished school, and they could get jobs in the silk mills of Paterson, New Jersey. Jacob had found a job in a bakery there, and had found a place for the three of them to live.

Again, it was time for some people to leave and for others to stay. There were hugs and kisses and a few tears. It was exciting and sad when Emmy and the rest of the family promised each other, "*Wiiderluege.*" There was something comforting about the Swiss-German word for good-bye. Emmy thought, "We will see each other again." Still, Emmy wasn't sure how she felt, so she didn't go into the house with *Grossmutti* and *Mutti* and her sisters Frieda and Marie. Instead she went into her grandmother's garden.

Chapter Seven

Emmy Emigrates to Amerika

Emmy lay in her grandmother's garden and looked up at the clouds. She imagined floating across the miles to see *Vatti* and her big sisters. She wondered what *Amerika* was like.

She wondered what it would look like when she got there. Letters from her father and sisters described the new home, but it was so hard to know what it was really like.

Then one day *Mutti* received a thick letter in the mail. She walked away by herself to read it and came back smiling through tears. Emmy felt strange. She couldn't tell if her mother was happy or sad.

Mutti called everyone together — *Grossmuetter*, Emmy, Frieda, and Marie. They sat around Mutti on the garden steps and listened to her read *Vatti*'s letter.

Emmy's eyes lit up when she heard it would soon be their turn to go. Then she looked at *Grossmutti* who sat with her face turned down. She looked at Frieda who looked pale, and at Marie who looked . . . who looked unsure. Emmy's mother had that sad-happy face. Then the light in Emmy's eyes grew dim. Emmy didn't know what to think.

The next day she saw *Mutti* trying to walk straight and tall. It was curious to see her practicing to walk without limping. Emmy wondered what happened. She knew it had something to do with the letter, and she knew Marie and Frieda could tell her, but they wouldn't talk about it to someone as little and young as Emmy.

Before too long, Emmy and the others gathered things together. *Grossmuetter Sekunda* gave her prayer book to *Mutti*. "Keep this close to your heart," the old woman counseled her daughter. "It will give you good messages, and it will remind you of me."

When all was ready, the travelers said, "*Uff Wiiderluege,* we'll see you again," to their friends and *Grossmutti*. They took the train to Basel where they changed to the train for *Cuxhaven* and rode out of Switzerland and across Germany to get to the seacoast. Luise tried very hard to look happy. She smiled as she opened the lunch Grossmuetter had packed — pieces of cheese, apples and . . . "Oh, goody, *Schänggeli!*" Emmy exclaimed.

At last they reached the seaport at *Cuxhaven*, located on the North Sea. *Mutti* found someone who could take them to the big ship, the "Amerika." It was on the Hamburg-America Steamship line.

Pulled up close to the dock, the "Amerika" was much larger than Emmy could have imagined. The body of the ship, called the "hull," sat near the top of the water that lapped gently between the hull and the pier. To Emmy, the ship was shaped something like the small boats she had seen on the Rhine River at Basel. It was pointy at the front and straight across the back. Later, she and her sisters would learn those parts were called the "bow" (pronounced as in "ouch") and the "stern." Around the top of the hull was a fence which was called a "railing." The floor, called the "deck," was flat inside the railing, making the deck look something like a porch on a house.

People were standing along the railing, waving and calling to their families and friends who stood — like Emmy and her family — on "the dock." Many of the people on the dock were there to wave good-bye to their families and friends. Others, as their mother was doing, gathered their families together, and walked to a ramp that had been put down from the deck to the dock. The ramp was something like a stair that they would have to climb to get up to the deck of the ship.

At the top of the ramp stood a ship's officer and a sailor welcoming the passengers to the ship "Amerika" that would be their home for the next ten days or so. Emmy felt excited and afraid all at once. Everything was strange, giving them promise of a new experience and a clear understanding that they were now leaving their former home behind.

Once they were on the deck of the ship, Emmy and her mother and sisters looked down at the dock and waving people. With *Vatti*, Louise and Sophie already in *Amerika* and *Grossmuetter* back at home, they knew there was no one from their family or village to wave and call good-bye to them. *Mutti* led her girls toward the bow of the ship where they found a place where they could look out onto the water. It was larger than any lake or river they had ever seen. Their mother told them it was called the "North Sea," and soon they would sail on the "Atlantic Ocean." Watching the waves roll in and out, and seeing only water out in front of them, was almost more than they could have imagined. Emmy called out to her mother, "*Mutti*, look at those white birds that are flying all around this ship!" As they all looked up at those strange birds with very round heads and hooked bills, *Mutti* said she had heard of them before. She said, "Seagulls are found wherever there are large bodies of water. The birds like to fly where people are because some give them bread and crackers to eat."

Then a loud blast of a horn on the ship told all of the people that the ship was getting ready to set sail. The sound was very deep and loud. It sounded again. Emmy could hear some people crying loudly. This was because they were sad to be calling good-bye to their loved ones.

Next, sailors hustled around and sent people to the sections of the ship where they would stay during their voyage. A few people would go through narrow doors, called "hatchways," to the place where their staterooms were located on the first level below the main deck of the ship. Most of the people, like Emmy and her family, would be sent toward the stern of the ship. Now they were taken down simple stairs far below the main deck and shown where they would sleep and live during most of the long trip.

As Emmy still stood on the main deck waiting her turn to go down, she looked up and saw smoke billowing from the large stack in the middle of the ship. The horn blasted again, and the ship, as it started to move, shuddered. Emmy then remembered their trip on the trains and how the piston and connecting rod worked on the engine to pull the trains. She could hear a big engine somewhere in the ship getting ready to take them out onto the ocean. She hadn't seen any tracks or a road when they had been looking out to the ocean. She wondered how the ship engineer would know where to travel to *Amerika*.

Emmy asked Frieda and Marie, "How does the ship engineer know how to get to *Amerika*?" When they shook their heads to show they did not know, a sailor standing nearby answered in German, "A man called a pilot uses a map and a compass to take us."

Emmy's eyebrows wrinkled together, and her eyes showed she was thinking. Then she asked the sailor, "What is a compass?" He explained it looks a little like a watch and has a needle that swings around to show the direction. The sisters thanked him. Emmy sighed with relief knowing the ship was in good hands.

Then Emmy and her mother and sisters started down the stairs, and it was their turn to find bunks and a spot where they would pass the time together.

Everywhere they looked were people who looked different, who dressed differently and who spoke differently. Emmy felt confused. They had to sleep in bunks below the ship's deck. They were not comfortable and clean like the beds they had at home. And always there was noise. Strange voices. Strange words. There were even strange smells of different foods. Emmy had never seen so many people. She thought, "There are even more people than in all of *Muttets*."

Mutti cried a lot even though she didn't want to do it in front of her children. She knew she would never see her mother again. Traveling took too long and cost too much money for most people to make many trips back and forth. It was very hard for *Mutti* who thought of how they had left her mother all alone.

Groups of people from the same countries gathered together. Some others stared around, or like *Mutti*, passed the time with their families. There were others, however, who were more outgoing.

As the days went by, once in awhile someone heard Emmy and her sisters speaking with each other. Because Emmy and her family spoke a language based on German, the people asked, "Are you German?"

Emmy always shook her head to one side and then the other and answered proudly, "No, we are Swiss!"

Finally, one day, after a time they thought would never end, they heard and then saw much commotion. People gathered their things and climbed up to the deck. Luise and her daughters hurried and picked up their things, too, and climbed the stairs. It was hard for Luise because of her legs, but they got to the deck and were able to squeeze closer to the railing.

Excitement was all around them on the faces and in the voices of others. Then they, too, saw the beacon of hope — the statue of the stately woman holding up the torch.

Someone said in English, "It's the Statue of Liberty!" Luise and her girls stretched to see the famous statue. She looked just as they had seen in pictures, but larger and more awesome. Then Luise looked over a little way and saw the large brick building. "There's Ellis Island!" she told her daughters. And they knew they would soon be seeing their father and sisters.

Chapter Eight

Emmy's Adventure on Ellis Island

Emmy's heart was beating very fast. Soon it would be their turn to get into the smaller ferry boat and go onto Ellis Island, *Amerika*.

The ferry took them into a narrow channel between the island with the Statue of Liberty and Ellis Island. People swarmed off the ferry. Emmy thought how strange it felt to be on land after all those days on the ocean. Workers tried to keep everyone in line, but some tried to rush ahead, and others shoved the ones in front of them. Luise thought, "These are not like Swiss people who are polite," while she kept her eyes on Frieda and blonde Marie. Emmy clung onto her mother's long coat.

As they stepped through the wide double doorway of the huge red brick building, they came to flagstone steps that would take them into the main part of the building. Although Luise felt the press of the crowd behind her, she was careful where she would step. She looked down at the steps in front of her and was surprised to see the grooves that many feet had already worn into the stone. Were these the very places on the steps that Jacob and their older daughters had placed their feet? Slowly Luise and her daughters walked to the landing at the stop of the stairs, and they followed others into The Great Hall.

As they entered, a worker wrote large black numbers on the identification tag pinned to Luise's coat. She was told she would have to listen for the number to be called. As they sat on their bench with their belongings piled around them, the girls gazed at the ceiling that was higher than any they had ever seen before. It made the ceiling in their Swiss church back home seem not high at all.

Emmy listened to the many voices talking at the same time. She said, "It sounds like a million bees." Their mother and Frieda and Marie agreed.

Just when Emmy's head hung down and she was beginning to sleep, their number was called, and they had to stand up and move to the line that was forming in another place. "Girls," Luise told them, "we will soon be walking in front of the inspectors. Please be very polite and do not say anything and do not ask me what I am doing."

Emmy wanted to ask why, but she could tell by her mother's stern voice that it was better if she said nothing. She looked ahead and saw the people in uniforms looking at everyone as they walked along in line. Some people had their eyes examined. Others had to open their mouths and stick out their tongues. Then Emmy looked at their mother who walked ahead of them, and she knew why Luise had been practicing walking at the grandmother's house. Just as their mother had warned, Emmy said nothing.

They walked past a woman who wore a white coat, similar to the kind a doctor might wear. She looked very closely at Luise and the three girls with the wide-brimmed straw hats who followed her. Emmy thought, "Maybe she notices our red hair." Then they passed on, and suddenly their mother seemed not to be as straight and tall. Unexpectedly, a voice called out loudly, "*Luisa, Luisa*, come back here." Luise turned and looked back at the woman in the white coat. She was now beckoning to Luise to return to her.

Luise looked surprised. She walked straighter and returned to the woman. "Lift your skirt, please, Luisa," ordered the woman. Then she called another woman over, who said in German, "Luisa, you will not be going to *Amerika* today. Please come with me."

Luise's shoulders sagged. She turned to her daughters and said, "Come, girls."

"No," said the German-speaking woman. "Not your daughters. Only you."

"*Aber, myni Kinder!* But my children! What will happen to them?" Luise pleaded. Emmy could tell their mother was very afraid. Certainly, so were Emmy and her sisters.

The woman's voice became softer, and she sounded kind. "Do not worry, *Luisa*. We will take care of them very well. You will not lose them."

Just at that moment another woman came and spoke in German to the girls, and they were taken to a room where other children and young people were gathered together. They were given sandwiches and some milk, and were told to try to get to sleep. They would not be entering *Amerika* that day.

Emmy, Frieda and Marie were frightened. They didn't understand what was happening. Would the people take their mother away and send her back across the ocean? What would happen to them? How could they go to sleep when they were too afraid even to take their straw hats off? But they were young and somehow managed to get some sleep, and before long, morning came.

They were lined up and taken to the Ellis Island dining room. It was a smaller hall than The Great Hall. Here there were lines of tables with benches next to them. The girls wondered what to do, but when the people ahead of them sat, they sat, too.

The people already at the tables were helping themselves to food from the dishes before them. Emmy looked across the table from her spot and saw two women wearing kerchiefs on their heads. They had sun-browned skin, and Emmy wondered what country they had come from. Suddenly, one of the women reached into the middle of the table, and grabbed a block of cheese — or was it butter? She broke it in half and gave half to her companion. They ate this food as though they had not eaten in many days and would probably not eat again soon. Emmy stared until she heard *Mutti*'s voice inside her head. "Do not stare at people. It is not polite."

Marie asked her two sisters, "What shall we do?" Emmy and Frieda couldn't answer. Just then a woman who heard them speaking recognized their dialect. So, in German she said, "*Mädchen,* you must eat. Help yourselves." Now that someone gave them permission, they selected their food. Once they had food in their bellies, they did feel better.

The workers at Ellis Island took good care of the children, and in another day or two, their father met the *Lüscher* girls and their mother. They were now on a big black train, much larger and dustier than Swiss trains. Soon they would all be together again with the rest of their family in their first home in *Amerika*.

Chapter Nine

Emmy Arrives at Her New Home

It was almost dark when they finally arrived in their new home in Paterson, New Jersey. Emmy's heart pounded. Their father had a surprise for them. He had bought a house with a bakery in it — just like home.

Their house was a tall three-story house with dormer windows on the top floor. It was at 41 Albion Avenue on which trolley cars clanged by during the day. When people got off at the corner of Albion Avenue and Henry Street, they often stopped at the bakery on their way home. The *Lüscher's* house was divided by an alleyway — a *Gässli*— from the house on the corner. In one direction, the straight street had one block more where it ended at a larger street. In the other direction, the street ran several blocks out of sight. Emmy wondered why their father wanted to leave their beautiful little Swiss village to come to such a big, crowded place. Of course, she was a child, so she had better not question.

The stairway inside the house was not quite as steep as the one at the end of the alleyway, leading to the second floor entrance. Jacob had thought correctly that Luise would find that inside stair a little easier to climb. He was sorry that he had found nothing where she wouldn't have to climb stairs at all, but that was hardly likely in any building with a bakery in it.

At the top of the stairs was a room that could be a sitting room or dining room. Unfortunately, there was only one window, and that was on the alley side of the house. On the other side was a small bedroom. With the kitchen behind the room and the living room in front, it promised to serve as a hallway more than anything else.

As they all sat around the kitchen table having their first meal together in a very long time, everyone seemed to be talking at once. After they had eaten, Jacob asked Luise to come with him to see the rest of the house, while their daughters continued to sit around the table sharing recent happenings.

Emmy's sisters Louise and Sophie told their three younger sisters what happened in Paterson while the others waited on Ellis Island. Louise told them, "*Vatti* went over to greet you on your first day in *Amerika*. He was very disappointed to be told to go home and get a sponsor so *Mutti* could come into *Amerika*."

"What's a sponsor?" Emmy asked. Marie and Frieda shook their heads. They didn't know what a sponsor was either.

Louise answered, "That is a person who agrees to pay for the doctor bills, if *Mutti's* legs get worse — and for her food, too. It has to be somebody who already lives in *Amerika* and has enough money. The people in charge of the country want to be sure everyone can take care of their own families."

The girls nodded, and Sophie continued the story. "*Vatti* was very angry. He wrote a long time ago to *Mutti* to practice walking straight and tall while she was still in *Muttets*. Now, because she had limped and they discovered the sores on her legs, he had to go that evening to some men from his Swiss club and see if there was anyone who could help him.

And then he had to return to Ellis Island the next day and the next.

"*Luggi* and I went to bed and I cried most of the night. Of course, in the morning I had to go to work. My eyes and face were all red from crying, and my forelady (supervisor) asked, 'What is wrong, Sophie? I expected to see you all happy and smiling, and here you are with a red face from crying!' Well, I explained to her about the sponsor. She looked sad and told me it was best for me to get to work so I could forget my unhappiness.

"Then, after awhile, the other girls who were working with me all looked up, and here came Mr. Brandis. He is the owner of the mill. We hardly ever see him, but this time, he walked right over to me and said, 'Sophie, I hear you are worried about your mother maybe being sent back to Switzerland. Well, you may stop worrying right now. I will be the sponsor for your mother.' I was so surprised, I could hardly speak, but I must have. He was smiling when he left me."

Louise then said, "So, the next day *Vatti* went over to Ellis Island with papers from two sponsors for *Mutti*. One was from the Swiss club and the other was the rich man who owned a big mill. So *Mutti* could come to *Amerika*."

Emmy asked, "Why does *Vatti* look so unhappy?"

Her two oldest sisters glanced at each other. It was Sophie who answered. "We knew how excited *Vatti* was that you would soon be here, and we know he missed *Mutti*. But then she forgot and limped at Ellis Island. When he couldn't pick you up on the first day, he had to go tell his friends what happened — well, you know *Vatti*. He felt very ashamed. He thought it made him look like a man who couldn't take care of his family."

They were sitting and wondering about this when their parents came back into the room. "Also," Jacob ordered, "do not sit around talking. Let's get the dishes done, and then off to bed. Tomorrow is a school day for Emmy and *Friedi*. Marie, you are now old enough to work, so I asked Sophie to take you to meet her forelady at Brandis Silk Mill. We'll all have things to do."

Emmy got up and helped carry the dishes to the sink, but she didn't say anything, knowing it was too impolite to speak back to her father. Besides, she was very interested in learning what her new school would be like.

Chapter Ten

Emmy Goes to School in America

The morning after they arrived in Paterson, Papa walked Frieda and Emmy the three blocks to school. The girls stared when they saw the large red brick building. It was so big! It had three floors and was surrounded by a concrete schoolyard. How different from their small stucco building in *Muttenz*! Their hearts felt heavy. Would they like going to such a big school? How many children would there be?

Their father entered the door and started walking down the hall where he saw a sign above a door that read "Office." He said, *"Aha, do isch s* office where my friend said we must come to see the principal." He and the girls entered. The woman he spoke with took them into Mr. Cassidy's office. The men shook hands and when *Vatti* told him these were his daughters, the principal looked at the solemn blonde-haired girl and at her red-haired sister. When he greeted them, Mr. Cassidy quickly realized the girls did not understand English, so he told their father it was best to place them in grades where they knew the subjects and could concentrate in learning the language.

Jacob said, "*Jo,* yes, I understand that. My daughters are smart girls, and you will see they are good girls, too. Thank you, Mr. Cassidy. I go now. I must get my pies ready."

Mr. Cassidy left Frieda at Miss Jackson's classroom. As he was taking Emmy to her room, he pointed to her and said, "Emmy, your name is Emmy." He pointed to himself and said, "My name is Mr. Cassidy." At first Emmy was unsure. She listened carefully and tried to understand what the principal was saying, but it was hard. When he repeated his action and words, the red-haired girl seemed to understand. She smiled and said, "You, Emmy. I, Misterr Kas ... a ... dee." The principal smiled and opened the classroom door.

Emmy stepped in and felt the eyes of thirty younger children staring at her. It was an awkward moment for her. She then followed the principal to Miss Wright's desk.

"Good morning, Miss Wright. I have a new student for you. This is Emmy. She comes from Switzerland. You will enjoy having her here." Though Miss Wright seemed nice enough, Emmy suspected the day would be confusing.

Once she was seated and the class work resumed, Emmy had a chance to get an idea of what was happening. Miss Wright walked to the board and took hold of a ring above the board. The ring was attached to a roll that looked like a window shade. Instead, she pulled down a map. Emmy heard Miss Wright say some words. Then she took a long stick pointer and pointed to Switzerland! All heads turned and looked at Emmy. She felt strange. Most of the girls looked friendly enough, but the boys' faces showed there was mischief behind them.

This caused Emmy to remember the time she had brought her pretend watch to school, and the boys got her so excited over it that she got into trouble. "Better be careful with these boys," Emmy thought.

Emmy saw something else that reminded her of school at home. When called upon, each pupil stood up and gave an answer. This was just the way they did it in Switzerland, but Emmy was really confused. This was a strange language, and she was expected to learn it. How hard it would be! But something happened that made her feel like there was hope.

Miss Wright called Emmy and a girl named Stephanie to her desk. They looked curiously at each other, and Miss Wright smiled. They made an interesting pair of children. Emmy's freckled skin was very fair to go with her red hair, and Stephanie's black hair and brown eyes matched her skin that turned brown in the sun. Miss Wright explained that Stephanie's parents came from Austria, a country next to Switzerland, so they spoke a dialect something like Emmy's.

"Stephanie, will you help Emmy learn our language? I'll move your seat next to hers."

Without doing a thing, Emmy had met her first American friend, who would be her friend for the rest of her life. So, much of the day went fairly well, and Emmy thought things would go all right.

Each morning Stephanie would walk the block from her house to the *Lüscher* Bakery to call for Emmy and Frieda. Then they walked the rest of the way together. Sometimes other children joined them, and Emmy and her sister slowly became friends with them.

It was in the classroom, though, where Emmy still felt uncomfortable. No matter how hard she tried to hide from Miss Wright's attention, she was called upon much more than the others. She hated it when Miss Wright asked her a question, and when Emmy stood trying to form the English words to give her answer, she'd feel hot and nervous. When the words finally came out — along with some Swiss words — there were always some giggles behind her. Although Miss Wright gave stern looks at the laughing children, Emmy still felt dumb.

But Emmy was not dumb. She was only one of many, many children all over America who were in classrooms learning to speak English. There was much for them to learn. Finally a day arrived when Emmy came home from school and told her family, "We're in America, and we can't call it '*Amerika*' anymore." She knew she was becoming an American. She felt like she belonged!

Chapter Eleven

Emmy Delivers a Cake

When Emmy's father left for America, he thought everyone easily could become rich in this country. As soon as he had saved enough money, with the help of his two oldest daughters, he had bought a new bakery. Now that the family was together again, they followed the custom they had in Europe. Everyone had to help. Even eleven-year-old Emmy was expected to do something.

One day when she came home from school and was ready to change her clothes and go out to play, Emmy's father called to her. She went into his office where he said, "Emmy, please take this birthday cake right over to Mrs. Roth's house. Do not stop to play. Make sure to hold the box tight and straight." So Emmy started off walking to Mrs. Roth's house with the birthday cake.

She did not stop to play with anyone, but her steps became slower and slower as she passed girls jumping rope and boys playing ball. She wished she could play, too. By and by, while she was watching some other girls jumping Double Dutch, Emmy forgot to watch the sidewalk, and she tripped over a crooked part of it. She stumbled, fell, and she dropped the cake.

The box flew open. The cake plopped right over and the icing stuck to the sidewalk. Emmy was so scared! What could she do now? Should she pick up the cake and put it back in the box and go back home? But she couldn't do that!

Vatti would be very, very angry with her. So, Emmy decided she would fix the cake. She looked at it and placed it in the box. The top of the cake looked just awful. The beautiful pink roses Papa had made were smushed and squished all over. Emmy got a stick and used it to scrape the dirt off the icing. That was much better, but it still didn't look very good. She had to do <u>something</u>! But she couldn't go back home!

Then she had a bright idea. She had a penny that her mother gave her when she started out on this walk to deliver the cake. Well, now she knew what she would do. Emmy was right in front of the ice cream store. She walked in and asked for a strawberry ice cream cone. Then she sat on the step outside of the store and she turned the cone upside down and smeared the ice cream all over the top of the cake. She tried to make roses like her baker father did. It was hard for her to do. At last she told herself. "It looks good!" She closed the box and stuck the rest of the ice cream cone into her mouth and chewed as fast as she could. Emmy walked very fast the rest of the way to Mrs. Roth's house. Emmy gave her the cake, and then hurried home. Once there, she changed her clothes and went out to play.

When it was time to go in for supper, Emmy walked into the house, and her father said in his low, loud voice, "Emmy, *kùmm do iine!* Come in here, Emmy! Now you tell me just what you did with Mrs. Roth's cake!"

Emmy shivered and Emmy shook, and Emmy swallowed very hard. Her head hung down and her voice was all soft and scared. She whispered, "I delivered it just like you said, *Vatti*."

His voice sounded just like thunder. "What did you do with the cake?" he yelled.

Emmy knew she had to tell the truth. She couldn't make up a story. She knew that her father knew what happened, so she answered, "Well, *Vatti*, I wasn't looking where I was walking, and I stumbled and dropped the cake. I didn't know how to fix it. So I cleaned off the icing and made new icing with ice cream." A tear dropped onto her cheek.

Jacob looked at Emmy, nodded his head and walked out of the room. He never said another word about Mrs. Roth's cake. After that, Emmy always walked very carefully when she delivered baked goods.

Chapter Twelve

Emmy Learns a Valuable Lesson

Not long after Emmy's cake-delivering nightmare, Marie was brought home very sick from her job. She was so weak and tired that she could hardly climb the stairs, even with Louise's help. *Mutti* asked what was wrong. Marie murmured, "My stomach hurts. I am so tired."

Mutti led Marie to bed and helped her undress. She soothed Marie's forehead and told her, "I will make you some chamomile tea. It will help the pain." When her mother returned with the tea, she found Marie asleep. Marie lay in bed without even her ever-present book for company. She was turned on her side with her legs drawn up to relieve the hurting.

When Marie awakened several hours later, *Mutti* brought cool, wet cloths to refresh Marie's hot forehead, and later, a hot cup of chamomile tea to warm her shivering body. The family tiptoed around and talked in low tones to keep from disturbing her. Two days passed, and Marie was no better.

Finally, when Marie awakened, whimpering with the pain, Papa declared that it was time to call *Der Dòggter*. These were the days when few people went regularly to doctors, who when asked, still made house calls. There also being few telephones in 1911, Sophie was sent to tell the doctor he was needed.

When the man with the black medicine bag arrived and was shown upstairs to examine sixteen-year-old Marie, *Mutti* continued reading from the prayer book her mother had given her. The anxious family waited together quietly until the doctor returned. "I have given Marie some medicine to relieve her," he said. "I'm sorry, there's nothing more I can do. It will be a matter of time."

After the doctor had left, Sophie's voice trembled. "Nothing he can do? Marie is too young to die!" Her face was flushed with frustration.

Vatti quieted Sophie. "*Söffi*, unfortunately doctors do not know how to fix everything. We must learn that each of us dies when it is our time. It is not for us to question God."

Vatti and *Mutti* went in to Marie. Soon, they brought her sisters in to see her. *Vatti* stepped to the foot of the bed, looking sadly down at his middle daughter. *Mutti* was seated on a straight-backed wooden chair with Sophie next to her. They looked much as they had when they posed for their official photograph many years before. As Emmy walked into the room, *Mutti* reached her hand toward Emmy who grasped it very tightly.

They felt comforting power flowing between them. Frieda knelt and held her beloved sister's hand in hers and hugged it to her. Louise stood nearby with tears streaming down her cheeks. She touched Marie's shoulder and quietly said, "Marie, we love you." Marie's skin was extremely pale, and she was very, very tired. She gave a faint smile and closed her eyes.

The pastor came to console the family. The next day the bakery was closed. As was the custom in Paterson, when most funerals were still conducted from home, there was an arrangement of white flowers nailed beside the doorway.

The custom allowed the family to tell the community they had lost a loved one. White flowers and ribbons meant it was a young person. The color purple was for an adult. A few neighbors, Swiss friends and fellow church members came to pay their respects. It was a sad time for the whole family.

For Emmy it had an extra-special meaning. When her sweet sister Marie was laid to rest in American soil, Emmy learned that there are worse things than dropping a cake. Losing her sister was one of them.

Chapter Thirteen

The Lüscher Bakery Gets a Delivery Truck

There was no one who worked harder than Jacob *Lüscher*. He made the best Swiss bread and the tastiest cinnamon-raisin buns in all of Passaic County. This did not satisfy Mr. *Lüscher*. He wanted all of New Jersey to know about his delicious baked goods.

More and more men were driving cars. So Mr. *Lüscher* bought a small bakery truck. It was hardly more than one of the new boxy, black passenger autos. It sat high off the ground upon very narrow tires. It had round lights, fixed separately, toward the front of the area where the engine was placed. Everything was simple. Nothing ornamental was on the vehicle.

Jacob went to the proper office to apply for a license tag and a driver's license. Now he was ready to maneuver his vehicle and deliver his wares to his customers on his bakery route.

Well, that was what Mr. *Lüscher* wanted to do. Instead, Jacob *Lüscher* steered to the right and steered to the left.

Other drivers shook their fists at him. "Get a horse!" they yelled. Horns blew.

"*Donnerwetter!* These people are rude," exclaimed Jacob. His face got red and hot. He felt so bad. He wanted to drive like all the other men, but no matter how he gritted his teeth and no matter how he bit his tongue, he could not drive straight down the lane.

So Mr. *Lüscher* advertised for a man to deliver his bread. The first one couldn't drive any better than Jacob. The second never came back after pay day. Another man couldn't speak English, so he couldn't talk with the customers.

"This is enough!" exclaimed Jacob. "*Friedi*, please come here!" he called. Frieda, a dutiful daughter, now a quite grown twenty years, stopped what she was doing. "Yes, Father?" she asked.

As she came farther into his office and walked to his desk, her father announced, "*Friedi,* you will drive our bakery truck."

Frieda drew a big breath. She looked at her father. Her eyes grew very large — just like saucers. "You want me to drive the truck and deliver the bread?"

Yes!" answered her father. Frieda said no more. She got a license. She climbed onto the running board, sat way up in the high seat, and drove the new truck right down the middle of the lane. The thin tires did not give her a smooth ride. Yet, it was less rough than wagon wheels would have been.

Emmy, who remembered the old tightrope days, said, "I'm not surprised. Frieda is determined, and she sure knows how to follow a straight line."

Frieda liked driving the truck, but she hated it when she was passing a group of men at ten whole miles an hour. "Hey, guys," one would yell, "wasn't that a woman driving that truck? Whoever heard of a woman driver?"

Frieda, who was the second woman driver in all of Paterson, New Jersey, closed her ears and blew the horn.

"A-goo-ga," the truck's horn called, "here comes the Bread Lady down the road."

Chapter Fourteen

Emmy and Stephanie have an Adventure

Emmy and her friend Stephanie had grown to be lovely young ladies. It was a warm, sunny Sunday afternoon, so they decided to go for a walk out toward the country. Since these were the days long before walking shoes or sneakers were popular — and the girls wanted to be fashionable — both of them wore their favorite dress shoes. Because she was older, Emmy's shoes were the more stylish with high heels and pointy toes.

Chatting and laughing, the two young ladies walked on and on. Finally, when they were very far out on Union Boulevard, they decided to sit on a boulder at the edge of a field. "Oh! My feet hurt," complained Emmy. "Do yours hurt, Steph?"

"Do they ever!" answered Stephanie as she pulled her shoes off. "M-m-m. That feels better," she added, wiggling her toes.

Although Emmy remembered she had been told her feet would swell in the heat and not fit back into her shoes easily if she removed her shoes, Emmy took hers off, too. Sure enough, when they decided to start back for home, they had to force their swelling feet into their rigid shoes. "Ouch! Will we ever make it?" Stephanie asked in some pain.

"Oh! I don't know," answered Emmy as she looked at her watch hanging on a chain around her neck. She had been so happy to receive that special birthday gift from Stephanie. She was thankful even now that she had it, but she had to turn her mind back to their hurting feet and getting home on time. "We have to make it! Our fathers will be furious if we're not home for supper."

So the two sadder, but wiser, young ladies hobbled step after step along the dusty road. At last they reached the cemetery and found a roadside bench to rest on. This time they tried to forget about their feet and their shoes. But forgetting was very hard with throbbing blisters to remind them. They watched an occasional Model T Ford bouncing down the road, and saw a few older walkers passing by wearing stout low-heeled shoes. All those people seemed happy from their walk and seemed to have no problem with their feet, so Emmy and Stephanie decided to continue on home. If they just didn't think of their aching feet, they really could make it.

Luckily for Emmy, she was wearing a broad-brimmed straw hat on top of her red-haired curls. It kept the sun from turning her fair-skinned face beet red. Now and then she took the hat off and fanned herself and Stephanie. When they realized they had walked only a few short blocks, they were discouraged and unhappy. Their feet still hurt and they needed to get home for supper. No more chatting or laughing as they dragged themselves along. The young ladies actually asked themselves if they'd ever be happy again. They paused and took a few deep breaths and shuffled onward toward home.

Suddenly, a Model T Ford coupe drove up. Two young men inside asked, "Hi, cuties, how about a ride home?"

Foolish as they had been about their aching feet, these well-brought-up young ladies drew themselves up, stuck their noses in the air and walked on. They had been cautioned by their parents not to go with strangers, strangers who might hurt or even kill them. Better to be alive with aching feet than dead with nothing to hurt them anymore.

The driver shrugged and drove on. His passenger looked out the back window and laughingly waved at them. Somehow, Stephanie and Emmy walked faster. They couldn't wait to get home. Hardly had the coupe gone out of sight when a motorcycle baroomed up to the curb. A policeman dismounted and came over to them. "Aren't you Herman's sister?" the uniformed man asked.

Stephanie's eyes widened in recognition. "Why, yes, Mr. Butler," she replied.

"Well, you two lovely ladies look pretty tired. How about if I give you a ride home?" They looked at each other, and did not have to be asked twice. After all, Mr. Butler was a friend of Herman's, Stephanie's brother, and he was a policeman.

"Come on, ladies, I'll help you into the sidecar. Just step up here, and in you go." Oh, it was so good to sit down again! The motorcycle's engine baroomed again, and off they went whizzing along the boulevard right past the two brazen fellows in the Model T Ford. The two young ladies laughed. Emmy had taken off her hat, and her hair blew behind her. The coolness was delicious!

They laughed again as Sunday strollers looked in disbelief at the motorcycle officer driving two young ladies in his sidecar. It was fun to forget their feet and enjoy all the attention.

At last they came to Albion Avenue. Mr. Butler turned the corner and stopped at Henry Street only a few steps from both of their homes. "Hurry home now," he told them as he helped them climb from the sidecar.

"Thank you, Mr. Butler," they chorused. "You saved our lives." The two friends giggled as they hugged each other and turned in the direction of their homes. What a great afternoon it had been! What an adventure to tell their co-workers about tomorrow!

# # #

As Emmy walked up the alleyway to the side door of her house, she reflected, "Maybe I'd be happier if we still lived in Switzerland, where everything is clean and beautiful and our old friends and family live, but it sure has been fun growing up in America!"

The End

Glossary

Foreign words sprinkled throughout **The Stories of Emmy** are Swiss-German, a language spoken by 74 percent of the Swiss population. The language has no official written form. Swiss-German is dear to the heart of each Swiss person who lives near Germany, Austria and Liechtenstein.

Unlike English, Swiss and German letters are often pronounced the same way in the different words they are used. For example, in English we have words spelled the same, but are pronounced differently. Take "cough" and "tough", "trough" and "through". The words have the letters in the same order, but each has a different pronunciation. Other words are spelled very differently, such as "their" and "there" and "so" and "sew." They have the same sounds, but very different meanings. The Swiss-German language does not have those confusing issues.

In Swiss-German, a vowel is pronounced the same each time. If there is a change in the sound of a vowel, there is often a character above the letter, such as two dots above the letter. When it is not possible to type the character above the letter, the letter is then combined with another vowel. The sounds are hard to describe in English, but I'll try to give you an idea of how to pronounce them, as I am attempting to familiarize you with the Swiss-German words, sentences or phrases used in the book. This is to give you a feel for the culture.

In Swiss-German, "a" is pronounced the same way each time. "A" is always said as "ah" in Swiss-German, unless there is an umlaut (ä — two dots — above it, pronounced "oom lout"). An "e" is always pronounced as the "e" in bed or end. The name "Emmy" is an example of "e" as in "bed." An "i" sounds like in the word "if". "O" is pronounced as in the word "oh". "U" always sounds like in the word "put," not like in "putt," so if the pronunciation says "MUT," it rhymes with PUT. The letter "j" is always said in Swiss-German as a "y" sound in English.

Combinations of letters also sound different in Swiss-German and American-English. My last name "Naundorf" is a good example. If it is being pronounced in Swiss-German or German, it would be pronounced "Noundorf" as in the American-English word "ouch." In our family in New Jersey we called it "Nawndorf," and still do.

Words, phrases and sentences are listed in alphabetical order by chapter, followed by the translation and then hints for American-English pronunciation.

Foreword

Basel. A large cultural city in northwestern Switzerland near Germany and France. This city spans the river Rhine. Historically Greater Basel was the richer side, and Lesser Basel was rather poor. "BAH-zl."

Baseldeutsch. An old Swiss-German dialect spoken in the city of Basel, Switzerland. "BAH-zl Dooch".

Emmy. Nickname for the little girl named Emma. "EM ee."

Grossmutti. Grandma. "grose MUT ee".

Heidi. A girl in the book **Heidi** by Johanna Spyri. "HI dee."

Mutti. Mommy. "MUT ee".

Vatti. Daddy. "VFAHT ee."

Chapter One – Emmy Picks Flowers

Auti. Short for automobile. "OUT ee."

Brieffdrääger. Letter carrier. "BREEF drag er."

Frau Frey. Mrs. Frey. "Frow FRAY."

Frau Tschudi. Informal name for Mrs. Tschudin as pronounced by Muttenz villagers. "Frow (t)CHEW dee."

Frau Tschudin. Formal name for Mrs. Tschudin. "Frow (t)CHEW deen."

Griessi Hèèr. Good morning, Sir. "GRI-e see HAIR."

Grossmutti. Grandma. "grose MUT ee".

Grossmutti Sekunda. Nickname for Emmy's grandmother, "Grandma Second," because she was the second girl born in her family. "grose MUT ee say **KOON** dah."

Grossmuetter. Grandmother. "grose MUT er."

Guete Daag. The greeting "Good day." "GOO-e te DAHG."

Guete Morge. The greeting "Good Morning." "GOO-e te **MORG**-e."

Jakob. Jacob. Emmy's father. "YA cohb."

Jo, de kasch go, aber de muesch zèèrscht no bim Grossmutti verbyy. Roughly translated, means "Yes, you may go, but you must first go to Grandma's house." "Yo de KAHSH go. Ahba de muesh tsairsht no bim Grose MUT ees **VER** bee." [Nobody said it would be easy!]

Jo, jo. Yes, yes. "YO, YO."

Luise. French way of spelling "Louise." "lew EEZ."

Maieryysli. Lilies of the Valley, flowers that bloom in May, having small white bell-like blossoms that are on delicate young twigs. "MY er **EEZ** lee."

Muttenz. Formal name for Emmy's village. "MUT enz."

Muttets. Informal name of Emmy's village as pronounced by villagers. "MUT ets."

Mutti. Mommy. "MUT ee".

Schäfer. A Swiss last name. "SHAY fer."

Schwaarz. Black. "shwahrts."

Vatti. Daddy. "VFAHT ee."

Chapter Two – Emmy's World Begins to Widen

Also, was hesch hütte vor? "Well, what is before you today?" or "Well, what are you planning for today?" "Also" is said as though a conversation has been going on, but is really in the speaker's thoughts. "UHL so, wahss heshh **HEWHTT-e** vfor?"

Dr Vatter hed klopft. Father has knocked. "der VFAHT er hed **KLOPFT**."

Elise. A girl's name. "ay LEES."

Frau Tschudin. Formal name for Mrs. Tschudin. "frow (t)CHEW deen."

Friedi. Nickname for a girl named Frieda. "FREE dee" and "FREE dah."

Grossmutti. Grandma. "grose MUT ee".

Guete Daag. The greeting "Good day." "GOO-e te DAHG."

Günther Ruedi. A boy's name. In Muttets, they say the family (last) name before the person's given (first) name. "GUNT her **ROO**-e dee."

Jo. "Yes." "YO."

Jo, das kasch mache. "Yes, you can do this." "YO dahs kahshh **MAHCHK**(clear throat)-e."

Johann Jacob Lüscher. Emmy's father's full name. "YO hahn YA cohb **LUHSH** er."

Luggi. Nickname for Louise. "LOO(g) kee."

Luggi und Söffi. Nicknames for Louise and Sophie. "LOO(g) kee und SUFF ee."

Muttenz. Formal name for Emmy's village. "MUT enz."

Muttenz bi Basel. Formal name for Emmy's village by the nearest city. "Bi" is dialect for the German "bei," which means "by." "MUT enz bee BAH-zl."

Mutti. Mommy. "MUT ee".

Söffi. Nickname for Sophie. "SUFF ee."

Vatti. Daddy. "VFAHT ee."

Werum? Nai, nai, Spätzli. "Why? No, no, sweetie." Spatzli is a diminutive form of Spatz. A Spatz is a sparrow. "wer OOM? NI NI **SHHPA** zli."

Zèèrscht duet me schaffe und noochhäär spiile. "First we work and later play." Noochhaar is similar to the English word "afterwards." "tsairsht doo et me SHAHF-e und **NUHCK**(clear throat) haar shpeeile."

Chapter Three – Emmy Goes to the Big City

Aeschevorstadt. A street in the city of Basel. "AHSH-e **VOR** shtat."

Arbogast. The name of a church built hundreds of years ago, during the Holy Roman Empire, for the Roman Catholic religion. During the 1500s, Muttets voted to change it to a Reformed Church. "AR boh gahst."

Auti. Short for automobile. "OUT ee."

Bääredrägg. Licorice. "BAAR(roll tongue)-e drak."

Clarastroos fümf. Five Clara Street. "CLAR ah strohs FUEHMF."

D'Wùùrscht. The sausage, as in liverwurst. "DWOOR-sht."

Danggerschehn. Thank you. "DONGK e shehn."

Dòchter. Daughter. "DOHCK(clear throat) ter."

Frau. Mrs. "frow."

Freii Strooss. The main street in Greater Basel. "FRI strohs."

Friedi. Nickname for a girl named Frieda. "FREE dee" and "FREE dah."

Gässli. Walkways between close houses, called alleyways. "GAS lee."

Grossmutti. Grandma. "grose MUT ee".

Gryyffegass. The main street in Lesser Basel when Emmy was small. Gryyffe is a bird of prey. "GREE fee guss."

Guete Daag. The greeting "Good day." "GOO-e te DAHG."

Günther Ruedi. A boy's name. In Muttets, they say the family (last) name before the person's given (first) name. "GEWNT her **ROO**-e dee."

Halt! Bitti, halt! "Stop! Please stop!" "HULT. BIT ee. HULT!"

Herr. High German for Mister (Sir). "hair."

Herr Carl Schmid. Mr. (High German) Carl Schmid. "hair KARL shmid."

Hildi. Nickname for Hilda. "HILL dee."

Jo, jo. Yes, yes. "YO, YO."

Luggi. Nickname for Louise. "LOO(g) kee."

Lüscher. Emmy's last name. "**LUHSH** er."

Maiteli. Small young girl. "MYT lee."

Mittleri Brugg. Middle Bridge. This historic bridge is older than Wettschtaibrugg and is a very important connection over the Rhine river between Greater Basel and Lesser Basel. "MIT ler BRU(g)K."

Münschterplatz. Munschter Place. This is the land around the cathedral. "MOON shter plahtz."

Muttenz. Formal name for Emmy's village. "MUT enz."

Muttets. Informal name of Emmy's village as pronounced by villagers. "MUT ets."

Mutti. Mommy. "MUT ee".

Schäfer. A Swiss last name. "SHAY fer."

Schmid. The last name Schmid. "shmid."

Söffi. Nickname for Sophie. "SUFF ee."

Vatti. Daddy. "VFAHT ee."

Wettschtaibrugg. Wetstone Bridge. It is a family name. This bridge is much more modern and north of Mittleri Bridge. "WET shti BRU(g)K."

Wiiderluege. See you again. The familiar German is "Auf Wiedersehen," meaning "until we see each other again," which is more formal than "Wiiderluege." "WEE der loo-eg-e."

Wilkùmme. Welcome. "WILL kuhm-e "

Willi. A man's first name. "WILL ee."

Yysebaan. Train station. Literally, the train and the rails. Tracks are referred to as "Eisenbahn" in German. Baseldeutsch is "Yse" instead of "Eisen." They both mean iron track. "EEZ-e bahn."

Zùùg. Train. "TSOOG."

Chapter Four – Emmy Tells the Time at School

Brieffdrääger. Letter carrier. "BREEF drag er."

dr Hèèr Lèèrer. Swiss-German dialect for Mister (Sir) Teacher. "der hair LAIR er."

Fritz. Boy's name. "frits."

Guete Morge. The greeting "Good Morning." "GOO-e te MORG-e."

Halber nyyni. "Half nine." In Britain, this means "half past nine," or 9:30, but in Germany and Switzerland it means "halfway to nine," or 8:30. "hulber NEW nee."

Hèèr Schaub. Mr. Schaub. "hair SHOUB."

Kinder. Children. (This where we get the name kindergarten.) "KIN der."

Jetz dien mr wider schaffe. "Now we will work again." "yetz deen mer WEE-i der **SHAHF**-e."

Was für Zyt? What time? "wahss fur TSEET?"

Was isch für Zyt, Emmy? What time is it, Emmy? "wahss ishh fur TSEET, Emmy?"

Chapter Five – The Circus Comes to Town

Anni. Annie. "**ANN** ee."

Bravo. Hooray! "Well done" in Italian. "Bravo!" is usually shouted at formal places like the opera. "brah VOH! brah VOH!"

Do kùnnt der Zirkus! "Here comes the circus!" "doh koont dair TSER koous."

Edelweiss. A European mountain flower. "AY-dl wice."

Fraulein. Miss. "FROY line."

Friedi. Nickname for a girl named Frieda. "FREE dee" and "FREE dah."

Handòòrgele. Small hand organ. An accordion. "hahnd ORG-e lee."

Hèèr Hans. Mr. Hans. "hair HAHNS."

Jakob. Jacob. Emmy's father. "YA cohb."

Lüscher. Emmy's last name. "**LUHSH** er."

Muttenz. Formal name for Emmy's village. "MUT enz."

Mutti. Mommy. "MUT ee".

Müller. A family name. "MUEH ler."

Seiler. A family name. "SY ler."

Chapter Six – Emmy Lives at Grossmuetter's House

Amerika. German for America. "ah MAIR i kah."

Grossmuetter. "Grandmother." "grose MUT er."

Grossmuetter Sekunda. "Grandmother Second," because she was the second girl born in her family. "grose MUT er say **KOON** dah."

Grossmutti. Grandma. "grose MUT ee".

Lüscher. Emmy's last name. "**LUHSH** er."

Muttenz. Formal name for Emmy's village. "MUT enz."

Mutti. Mommy. "MUT ee".

Schäfer. A Swiss last name. "SHAY fer."

Schänggeli. A special Swiss dessert that is not very sweet. It is shaped something like a fat finger. Wonderful for dunking! "SHANGK-eh lee."

Vatti. Daddy. "VFAHT ee."

Wiiderluege. Short for "See you again." Literally, "Look at you again." "WIEE der LOO-eg-e."

Chapter Seven – Emmy Emigrates to Amerika

Amerika. German for America. "ah MAIR i kah."

Cuxhaven. Seaport in Germany located on the North Sea. "CEUKS hahv en."

Grossmuetter. "Grandmother." "grose MUT er."

Grossmuetter Sekunda. "Grandmother Second," because she was the second girl born in her family. "grose MUT er say **KOON** dah."

Grossmutti. Grandma. "grose MUT ee".

Muttets. Informal name of Emmy's village as pronounced by villagers. "MUT ets."

Mutti. Mommy. "MUT ee".

Schänggeli. A special Swiss dessert that is not very sweet. It is shaped something like a fat finger. Wonderful for dunking! "SHANGK-eh lee."

Uff Wiiderluege. See you again. The familiar German is "Auf Wiedersehen," meaning "until we see each other again," which is more formal than "Wiiderluege." "WIEE der loo-eg-e."

Vatti. Daddy. "VFAHT ee."

Chapter Eight – Emmy's Adventure on Ellis Island

Aber, myni kinder! But my children! "ah ber, my nee KIN der!"

Amerika. German for America. "ah MAIR i kah."

Luisa. U.S. government inspector's way to say Luise's name. "lew EE sa."

Lüscher. Emmy's last name. "LUHSH er."

Mädchen. Young ladies. "MAYD ken."

Mutti. Mommy. "MUT ee".

Chapter Nine – The Lüscher Bakery Gets a Delivery Truck

Amerika. German for America. "ah MAIR i kah."

Friedi. Nickname for a girl named Frieda. "FREE dee" and "FREE dah."

Gässli. Walkways between close houses, called alleyways. "GAS lee."

Luggi. Nickname for Louise. "LOO(g) kee."

Lüscher. Emmy's last name. "**LUHSH** er."

Muttets. Informal name of Emmy's village as pronounced by villagers. "MUT ets."

Mutti. Mommy. "MUT ee".

Vatti. Daddy. "VFAHT ee."

Chapter Ten – Emmy Goes to School in America

Aha! Do isch s. Aha! Here is the . . . "aha! doh ishh s." (The letter 's' is part of an understood word "das.")

Amerika. German for America. "ah MAIR i kah."

Jo. Yes. "YO."

Lüscher. Emmy's last name. "**LUHSH** er."

Muttenz. Formal name for Emmy's village. "MUT enz."

Vatti. Daddy. "VFAHT ee."

Chapter Eleven – Emmy Delivers a Cake

Kùmm do iine. Come in here. "kuhm doh EE na."

Vatti. Daddy. "VFAHT ee."

Chapter Twelve – Emmy Learns a Valuable Lesson

Der Dòggter. The Doctor. "dair DOGK ter."

Mutti. Mommy. "MUT ee."

Söffi. Nickname for Sophie. "SUFF ee."

Vatti. Daddy. "VFAHT ee."

Chapter Thirteen – The Lüscher Bakery Gets a Delivery Truck

Donnerwetter! Thunderstorm or thunderweather, an expletive that shows annoyance. "**DUN** ner WAT er."

Friedi. Nickname for a girl named Frieda. "FREE dee" and "FREE dah."

Lüscher. Emmy's last name. "**LUHSH** er."

CPSIA information can be obtained
at www.ICGtesting.com
Printed in the USA
BVHW031152050820
585556BV00001B/56